Lectures on the Tinnevelly Missions

ROBERT CALDWELL

1857

TABLE OF CONTENTS

INTRODUCTORY LECTURE

The possessions which have fallen to the lot of the English nation in India are the most valuable and important that any people has ever acquired beyond its own natural boundaries. India comprises nearly a million and a half of square miles, an area which is equal to the half of Europe, leaving out Russia ; and, though nearly two-thirds of the soil are uncultivated, so thickly peopled are the cultivated districts, that the population of India amounted, in 1851, to 171,859,055 (more probably to 180,000,000 at least,) a population which is twice as great as that of the corresponding area in Europe, and which constitutes nearly a quarter of the whole population of the world.

The smallness of the number of the English in India is very extraordinary, and is a fact which is full of significance. The whole of the inhabitants of India are either directly under British rule, or they are inhabitants of " native protected states," in which all proceedings of importance are controlled by a British " Resi dent ;" yet the English in India, to whom the government of 180 millions of Hindiis has been committed, do not number 60,000 souls ! The proportion subsisting between the English and the native population, in some of the older provinces of British India, is especially extraordinary. For example, in Tinnevelly and Madura, the two most southern " collectorates," or provinces, in the Madras Presidency, amongst a population of more than, three millions, the number of Europeans, including civilians and mili tary men, Missionaries and merchants, men, women, and children, is under 300, and the Europeans who are directly engaged in the work of government, or in that of coercion, in those two provinces do not number a hundred altogether ! It might almost be regarded as a miracle that so many should submit to the government of so few ; but, what renders it more remarkable is, that they have hitherto submitted to it, not reluc tantly, but peaceably and contentedly. The people of those pro vinces, as of all the old settled provinces of Southern India, are more easily governed than the inhabitants of any county in England. There is only one regiment, and that a regiment of Sepoys, officered by Englishmen, in the two provinces referred to, amongst a population greater than that of Scotland ; and the services of that one regiment have not been required for anything more serious than routine duty since 1809!

It has often been said that our rule in India rests upon military force ; but recent events have proved that it depends far less upon force than upon opinion. It rests partly on the opinion of the in vincibility, in the long run, of the English arms and policy; but in a much greater degree it rests on the opinion which the Hindus, as distinguished from the Mahometans, every where entertain, that the English Government, whatever be its faults, is the best government India has seen for many generations ; not equal, indeed, to the paternal governments of the mythical golden age, but more than equal to any government that these prosaic times have heard of. It is a mistake to suppose that the Hindus feel towards the English the soreness of a conquered people. Those of them who know anything 'of the history of their nation prefer to represent matters thus: " The English never deprived us of any power or privilege of which they found us in the possession ; they rescued us from the tyranny of our Mahommedan conquerors ; and in all their early battles we fought with theia, sMe by side, not against them. "VVe arc convinced also, that if the English were driven from the country, it would be a loss, not a gain, to us Hindus ; for the Mahommedans would again get the upper hand, and they would give us a far smaller share in the government of our own country than we now enjoy, besides treating us and our religion with a harshness and bigotry of which the English have never shown any trace." Occasionally, it is true, the Hindus indulge in the popular English practice of grumbling, and not without reason, for the pressure of taxation is in some districts extreme, and the adminis tration of justice is still very defective ; but, in so far as the latter particular is concerned, it is not the English, but their own country men, that are blamed, for the fault lies with the subordinate officials, who are in variably natives; and the remedy which Hindus themselves would propose, and which I have heard many of them propose, is not the expulsion of the Europeans, but such an increase in their number as would enable them to make their influence felt in every corner of the country. Mainly and ultimately, however, I doubt not that the rule of the English in India rests neither on force nor on human opinion, but on the will of the Most High, the Supreme Ruler of the nations, who has raised up England, and confided race after race and region after region to her care, that she might " tell it out amongst the heathen that the Lord is King." It cannot be supposed that Divine Providence has placed England in so high a position, and brought about such extraordinary results, for no other purpose than our national aggrandizement: it was surely for the benefit of India that He permitted us to become the rulers of India, it was in order that we might impart to India the benefit of our just laws, our rational liberty, and our progressive civilization, and especially that we might impart to it the know ledge of the religion of Christ that religion which alone can make any nation good, happy, or permanently great.

Our duty, as a Christian Church and nation, to promote the religious welfare of India has generally been admitted ; but until our slumbers were rudely disturbed by the recent Mutiny and the dreadful proofs that were furnished by heathens and Mahome tans that bad religions are worse than none, that duty was not sufficiently recognised in this country, and certainly was not sufficiently felt, even by religious people. An encouraging amount of interest in the progress of Christianity in India has now at last been awakened, and a demand for information has been excited: it is now felt that a great door and effectual has been opened to us in India, and that the conversion of India to Christ is one of the greatest works, if not the great work, to which the Church and nation of England are called. I proceed, therefore, to give some idea of the present position of the Christian cause in India, espe cially in the Presidency of Madras.

Those who are acquainted Avith India, or who bear in mind the numerous and very peculiar difficulties with which Indian missions have to contend, will not expect me to paint a rose-coloured picture of missionary progress. Progress undoubtedly has been made, and year by year the prospects of Christianity become more encourag ing ; but the encouragements are of such a nature as will best be appreciated by those whose experience in some work similar to this has taught them not to " despise the day of small things."

Only one generation has elapsed since our Christian Govern ment systematically refused permission to Missionaries to labour in India, and openly patronised heathenism. It administered the affairs of all the more important pagodas, and compelled its ser vants to do honour to heathen festivals. I have myself seen idols that had been erected by its European servants, and wholly at its expense. As might naturally be expected in so unprincipled an age, the immoral lives of most of the English then resident in India was a scandal to the Christian name, insomuch that it became a proverbial expression that they had left their consciences at the Cape of Good Hope. We have reason to be thankful that a very different state of things now prevails. The character of the English in India has wonderfully improved, especially within the last thirty years, and the Indian Government itself has parti cipated in the improvement. Some improvements (especially that very important one, the severance of the connexion between the

Government and the idolatries of the country,) were effected by a prandlt; i ;-sure from without; but the greater number of improvements, including all that have taken place within the last fifteen years, have originated with the Government itself, which now comprises a considerable number of right-minded Christian men. The Indian Government has always professed to observe a strict neu trality between Christianity and heathenism, and to allow every religion professed by its subjects "a fair field and no favour;" but whatever may have been its professions, for a long period the only neutrality it observed was a one-sided neutrality, which showed itself in the encouragement of heathenism, and in oppo sition to the propagation of Christianity. This unfair, unright eous course has been almost entirely abandoned ; the Government no longer actively befriends heathenism, it no longer guards against the progress of Christianity as a source of danger. It still, indeed, professes to stand in a neutral position, but this neutrality has for some time been verging (perhaps as rapidly as is compatible with the circumstances of India) into an enlightened, prudent solicitude for the peaceful diffusion of the blessings of Christian education and morals. The burning of widows and female infanticide have been put down, slavery has been abolished, in connexion with all Government business and public works, Sunday has been made a day of rest, converts to Christianity have been protected, by a special enactment, in the possession of their property and rights, the re-marriage of widows has been legalized, female education has been encouraged, a comprehensive scheme of national edu cation has been set on foot, in connexion with which the Grant- in-Aid system has been introduced, and Missionary schools are no longer excluded from the benefit of Government Grants.

The Indian Government moves forward slowly, but it keeps constantly moving it takes no step backwards and hence, notwithstanding its characteristic caution, perhaps there is no government in the world which has made greater progress, within the time specified, in moral and social reforms. Undoubtedly much remains for the Government to do before it can be admitted that it is doing its duty to God and to India ; but I hope and believe that the unparalleled trials through which it has been called upon to pass will end, not in deterring it from its duty, but in urging it forward in the course of pimrovement.

Whilst we are thankful that the Indian Government, as such, has improved so considerably, we have also much reason to be thankful for the improvement which has taken place in the lives of so many members of the Anglo-Indian community. It is true that many members of that community are far, very far, from being what they ought to be, but at the same time it will be difficult to discover anywhere more Christian piety, in proportion to the numbers of the community, than amongst the English in India. In every district, in every station, with which I am acquainted, there has been a succession of men who have distin guished themselves, not only by their gentlemanly honour and by the purity of their lives, but by their Christian benevolence and zeal ; and such persons render most important aid to the cause of Missions, not only by their sympathy and contributions, but still more by the influence of their example. Whilst the Missionary is preaching Christianity to the Hindus, many an English layman is exemplifying to the Hindus what Christianity means: without abandoning " the calling wherein he was called," or violating any principle of official propriety, he is proving to a regiment or to an entire province that the teaching of the Missionaries is true, that Christianity is only another name for a holy and useful life, that it must have come from God, because it makes men godly, and that is an argument which every man can understand and appre ciate, and which no man can gainsay. Now that teachers of Christianity have free access to every part of India, the old assertion that the conversion of the Hindus is impossible has been proved to be a fable. In many instances the impossibility has been accomplished. It is quite true that in many extensive districts the work has not yet been begun, and that in no district have all the results that have been aimed at been accom plished ; but enough has been accomplished to prove to us that the work is of God, and to encourage us to go forward in it with vigour.

We cannot expect in India or anywhere, to " reap where we have not sown, or to gather where we have not strawed:" desultory efforts in too wide a sphere cannot be expected to produce the same results as systematic persevering labours within manageable limits j but when we find, wherever we look in India, a propor tion existing between labour and the results of labour, when it is evident that there is most success where there is most labour, and least success where there is least labour, 1 think we have every reason to thank God and take courage.

A comparison of the spiritual condition of the three Indian Presidencies will illustrate the proportion existing between efforts and results. In the Presidency of Bombay least has been done: the Society for the Propagation of the Gospel has not a single missionary labourer there, and other missionary Societies have but a small handful of men; and in that Presidency I am sorry to say that there are not a thousand native Protestant Christians from Goa to the Indus. In the Presidency of Bengal the number of Missionaries is more considerable ; and there, not only are the Christian converts seventeen or eighteen times more numerous than in Bombay, but in many parts of that vast Presidency the Hindu mind has been stirred to its inmost depths by the progress of Christian education and Christian civilization.

It is in the Presidency of Madras, however, that there has been the largest amount of missionary effort. Missionaries have been labouring in several parts of that Presidency for a considerable period ; their number bears some proportion to the work which they are endeavouring to accomplish, and is such as to render it possible for them to work in combination. What progress, then, has been made in that Presidency ? Not all the progress, indeed, which we wish for and hope to see, but still an amount of progress which is very encouraging. In the Presidency of Madras there are at least 80,000 native converts from heathenism, in connexion with the different Protestant Missionary Societies at work in various parts of the field, and of that number about 58,000 are connected with the Missions of the Church of England. Doubt less, many of the native Christian converts are not what we should wish them to be ; and much, very much, remains to be done before Christianity is diffused throughout the Presidency ; but it would be most ungrateful, as well as unreasonable, to ignore the fact that much has been done already, and that we have received encouragement to attempt, and to expect to accomplish much more.

Indian Missions may be divided into two classes: viz. the educational, or those which endeavour to reach the higher classes by means of superior English schools ; and the popular, if I may use the expression, or those which endeavour to reach the com munity at large (though practically, in most instances, they reach the lower classes alone) by means of vernacular preaching and vernacular education. The great English schools, or colleges, established in Madras, Calcutta, and Bombay, by the Scotch Presbyterians, stand at the head of the former class ; at the head of the latter, which includes almost all other missionary efforts, we may safely place the Missions of the Church of England in Tinnevelly.

It cannot be doubted that the endeavour to diffuse Christianity amongst the higher classes of the Hindus is one of very great importance, for the institution of caste gives the higher classes greater influence in India than in any other country ; but from Swartz's time till very recently, nothing was done for them by any missionary Society. They could not be reached, at all events they were not reached, by any of the agencies formerly at work ; and up to the present time it is only by means of an English educa tion of so high an order as to be an attraction to them, that those classes have, in any degree, been brought within the range of Christian influences. This plan originated with Dr. Duff and the Scotch Presbyterians ; and in the great schools which have been established by them, and more recently by some other Missionary Societies in some of the principal Indian cities, not only the science and literature of the western nations, but also the truths of the Christian religion, are daily taught by men of the highest ability to thousands of the most intelligent of the Hindu youth. This educational system had only just been introduced into Madras when I arrived, in 1838, and had not yet borne fruit ; but about a hundred persons belonging to the higher ranks of Hindu society have now been brought by it into the Christian fold. It is true that this number is very small, compared with that of the converts connected with the other system of Missions ; but it is to be borne in mind that they belong to a very influential class, a class in which no other system of means has borne any fruit whatever ; and that, as the converts of this class have had to fight their way to Christ through many persecutions, many of them have risen to a peculiarly high standard of Christian excellence and devoted- ness. It is a very interesting circumstance, that through the influence and example of this class of converts, Christianity has begun to spread amongst persons belonging to the same social rank who have never been at any missionary school at all, or who have been educated at Government schools from which Christian teaching is carefully excluded ; and it would appear that in Calcutta this new cfass of converts is now more numerous than the former. It is also chiefly owing to the influence of English education that so many social reforms are now making progress amongst the higher classes of the Hindus. This educational department of missionary effort is far from being the only one which claims our sympathy, as some of its advocates appeared at one period to suppose ; but it is certainly one of very great importance ; and I may be permitted to say that it does not seem very creditable, either to the English people or to the Church of England, that the Scotch Presbyterians have been allowed almost to monopolize the Christan education of the higher classes of the Hindus. The Church of England is, un doubtedly, doing a great work in the rural districts ; and in Benares, Masulipatam, Palamcottah, and a few other places, the Church Missionary Society has established English schools for the higher classes ; but it is much to be wished that the English Church put forth more of her strength in the cities the seats of government and commerce, and contribute, what she has not yet done, her full share of effort towards the Christianization of the high-caste Hindus. The inequality at present existing is to be rectified, not by other bodies of Christians doing less, but by the Church of England doing more.

The Socidi/for the Propagation of the Gospel was a" few years ago, led by such considerations to establish a Mission for the higher classes in Delhi a Mission which has for the present been quenched in blood, but which, I trust, will ere long be revived. More re cently still the Society resolved, at the representation of the pre sent excellent Principal of Bishop's College, Calcutta, to make that institution useful, not only for the training up for the ministry of those who are already Christians, but for the still more necessary work of converting educated heathens to Christianity. In the Presidency of Madras it has not yet done anything in this direction, though it has three institutions for the training up of catechists, schoolmasters, and native ministers ; but T trust it will not be much longer the only great Missionary Society in that Pre sidency which leaves to their fate the higher classes of the heathen youth. The Vepery Mission Grammar Scfrool, an institution established by this Society for the education of the Indo-British youth, did much for the improvement of that class, at a time when no other Society did anything. That school has fulfilled its mission, and has now ceased to exist ; but I hope that something will be established in its room, more directly tending to the diffu sion of Christianity amongst the heathen. A few years ago I would have pleaded for the establishment in the same buildings of a thoroughly good English school, for the benefit of the Hindu youth, to be taught, not by ordinary schoolmasters, but by thoroughly qualified, devoted English Missionaries ; but at present what appears to be more urgently required, what appears, indeed, to be the great want of all the Presidential cities at present, is an organized system of means for bringing Christian influences to bear upon the minds of those Hindus who have received a superior English education already, either in Missionary or in Government schools, but who still continue heathens. This class of persons may be numbered by thousands ; and every mem- fcer of the class can be reached through the medium of the English tongue. Here is a promising door of usefulness standing open, an extensive and rich field of labour lying vacant: which Society will have the honour of first entering in 1

The other class of Missions, the popular or parochial, as distin- guished from the purely educational, expend much money and effort on education, especially on the education of the children of the poorer classes in the vernacular languages ; but they may properly be regarded as acting on a different system, inasmuch as they labour for the benefit, not of the young only, but of the people at large ; and the schools which they establish are con nected with, and subordinated to, Christian congregations. With the exception of a few hundred at most, the entire body of native Christians may be claimed as the fruit of this system, which has been much more productive than the other of present, visible results.

In the city of Madras itself, there are about 2,600 converts of this class in connexion with the various Protestant Missions ; but when we leave the Presidency and travel southwards, we shall find a much greater number in almost every province.

In the rich and populous province of Tanjore, in connexion with the Missions of the Society for the Propagation of the Gospel which were founded by the venerable Swartz, there is a native Christian community, comprising about 5,000 souls ; and about half that number are connected with the revived Lutheran (Leipsic) Mission of Tranquebar. In those old Missions, Christian life and missionary zeal had sunk to a low point, in consequence of the retention of caste distinctions ; but within the last fifteen years the Gospel Propagation Society's Mission in Tanjore has been greatly purified and invigorated. The parochial system has been introduced, and the native congregations brought under efficient superintendence ; education has made rapid progress ; one of the best training seminaries in the country has been brought into operation: caste, the source of so many mischiefs, has been repressed ; and though, in consequence of these refor mations, especially in consequence of the systematic discourage ment of caste, the numbers of the Christian community have been diminished, the gain to the Christian cause has been more than equivalent.

Further south, in the adjacent province of Madura, a province peculiarly rich in historical associations, the American Board of Missions, a Presbyterian and Congregationalist Society, has occu pied the field in great force. I remember the commencement of that Mission, and happened some years after to travel through the province. At that time not a single convert had been made. On returning to this country three years ago, on my way from Tinnevelly to Madras, I again passed through the district occupied by the American Mission, and found that the number of native converts had increased in the intervening period from nil to between 4,000 and.5,000. The interesting and hopeful move ment which is going forward in that province appears to have originated in the influence of Tinnevelly Christianity. This was admitted by the American Missionaries themselves, and two of their number were deputed a few years ago to visit Tinnevelly, and go from station to station, for the purpose of making them selves acquainted with the details of our Missionary system. In the same province there are several old congregations connected with the Gospel Propagation Society, and an interesting offshoot from that Mission has recently been established amongst the Poliars of the Pulney Hills, a poor, long-oppressed, simple- minded race, to whom the reception of the Gospel has been as life from the dead.

On the western side of the Ghauts, the great mountain-range of Southern India, Christianity is also making progress. The Missionaries of the Basle Missionary Society have been labouring for the last twenty years in the provinces of Malabar and Canara, on the Malabar coast, and when I last heard of their progress, their converts from heathenism amounted to 2,000. Further south, on the same coast, there are the interesting Missions of the Church Missionary Society in the native states of Travancore and Cochin. I have not been long enough in India to remember the commencement of those Missions, but I have twice visited their principal stations, and on the occasion of my second visit, after an interval of nine years, I found both the number of Missionaries and the number of the native Christians under their care nearly doubled. It was particularly gratifying to find that the new converts who had been gathered in were not like the first converts, proselytes from the Syrian Church an old and interesting, though corrupted, Christian communion, but were direct acces sions from heathenism, especially from classes of heathens that had never before been reached. Amongst those newly-reached classes are the "Hill-kings," a race of rude, aboriginal moun taineers, living mostly in trees, and rarely before seen by any European eye. The Church Missionary Society's Missions in those districts comprise nearly 6,000 converts, who have to con tend with greater difficulties than any other native Christians in southern India, in consequence of the heathenism of the Malayala people being the most intense and fanatical with which I am acquainted, and the government of the country being heathen.

Further south still, in the Tamil portion of the Travancore country, are the Missions of the London Missionary Society, the most important and successful Missions of that Society in India, and which in the list of Indian rural Missions rank next to those of the Church of England in Tinnevelly. In connexion with those Missions there are upwards of 18.000 converts to Christianity, nearly all of whom speak the same language as our own converts in Tinnevelly, belong to the same castes and classes, and may be regarded as the same people ; and though in point of numbers they are considerably behind our Tinnevelly Christians, yet in education, public spirit, missionary zeal, and liberality in contributions to charitable objects, they have made, in proportion to their numbers, at least equal progress.

I now come, last of all, to Tinnevelly, the province in which it was my own privilege to labour during the greater part of my Indian life. Tinnevelly is the most southern province on the Coromandel coast) lying immediately to the south of Madura, and though a peculiarly hot, sandy, and unattractive region, it claims to be regarded by the Christian with pecxiliar interest ; for there the eye and heart wearied elsewhere with proofs of the power and prevalence of heathenism are gladdened by the sight of the largest, the most thriving, and the most progressive Christian community in India. The only Missions anywhere in the East which are said to be equally or more progressive, are those of the American Baptists amongst the Karens in Burmah ; but as I am not personally acquainted with those Missions, I am unable to say whether this representation is correct. In the subsequent Lectures I hope to describe more fully the Missions in Tinnevelly; it will suffice at present to say, that in that province alone, through the united instrumentality of the Church Missionary Society and the Society for the Propagation of the Gospel, 20 missionary dis tricts have been formed, and 43,000 persons men, women, and children rescued from heathenism and brought under Christian instruction ; and that now, amongst other signs of approaching maturity, considerable progress is being made by the native Church towards the support of its own institutions without foreign aid. It is true that much remains to be done before our Christian community in Tinnevelly is in all respects worthy of the Christian name, and that there, as elsewhere, Christian pro fession and public spirit are not always accompanied by personal piety ; but it is necessary, and very consolatory, to bear in mind that in what has already been accomplished there is much reason for thankfulness, and that the degree in which old things have already passed away is an encouragement to us to hope that in due time all things will become new.

In one of my subsequent lectures I will endeavour to give a fair estimate of Hindu Christianity, and to prove that, whatever be its defects, it includes a large amount of real sincerity; but I may here remark, that the liberality with which the religious members of the Anglo-Indian community contribute to missionary purposes is a pleasing testimony to the reality of the work which is going forward. Though the English in India do not number more than 60,000 souls, the great majority of whom are private soldiers, the average amount contributed in India for the promotion of missionary objects has been estimated at about 40,OOOZ. per annum. The list of contributors will be found to include the names of many judges and magistrates, heads of departments and governors, men of high official standing and of long Indian experience, who testify, not only by their contri butions, but oftentimes by their counsel and co-operation, their estimate of the importance of the work. There is something in structive also in the proportionate amount of their subscriptions. If the eye runs down a list of Anglo-Indian contributors to any missionary or charitable object, more donations of 100 rupees (10Z.) will be discovered than of sovereigns in this country.

It is an interesting feature of real missionary work everywhere, and certainly not less so in India than in other parts of the world, that it is carried on with so small an admixture of party- spirit. In Tinnevelly, for example, we may confidently say, " Behold how good and joyful it is for brethren to dwell together in unity." Generally, the Society for the Propagation of the Gospel and the Church Missionary Society have chosen different and distant spheres of labour, the former labouring chiefly in the Colonies, the latter exclusively amongst the heathen; but in India the spiritual care of our own countrymen being provided for by the East India Company's Ecclesiastical Establishment, aided by the efforts of Additional Clergy Societies, the Society for the Propagation of the Gospel is set free to labour, like the younger Society, amongst the heathen alone; and in Tinnevelly, the Mis sionaries of both Societies labour not only in adjacent districts of the same province, but in one and the same department of work. Under these circumstances some antagonism or jealousy might possibly have been apprehended ; but so far from anything of the kind having appeared, I only wish that all Christ's ministers in this country were labouring in their Master's cause with anything like equal harmony and brotherly cordiality. Two Bishops of Madras, the Bishop of Calcutta, and the Bishop of Victoria, observed, and recorded their gratification in observing, the good feeling which existed, and the last public expression of that feeling which took place before I left Tinnevelly was one which was peculiarly interesting to myself. The Missionaries and a few European catechists of both Societies met in my house for prayer and conference, and for the transaction of business connected with various societies which are supported in common; and on that occasion I had the pleasure of receiving twenty-eight guests, of whom nineteen belonged to the Church Missionary Society, and nine to the Society for the Propagation of the Gospel. Seven of the guests were native clergymen. Whatever differences exist, or are supposed to exist, between the two Societies, they relate, not to actual missionary work, but to preliminaries ; and when once those preliminaries are settled, when Missionaries of either society have actually been appointed to a station, and their work is commenced, no appreciable difference remains. All labour alike under epis copal superintendence, with the same purpose in view, in the same spirit, and in substantial conformity to the same principles of action. The only strife which I ever observed between the two Societies was of a friendly, Christian sort, which conduced greatly to the advantage of both. C. M. S., with her larger body of Missionaries, and her boundless finances, would always endeavour to outstrip S. P. G. ; and poor S. P. G., though sadly crippled by poverty and even by debt, would always endeavour not to be outstripped.

It is not only, however, with respect to the mutual relations of the two great Societies of the Church of England that party- spirit has been successfully repressed in India ; it has been re pressed within much wider limits.

In this old Christian country, the church of Christ, the com munity of baptized believers, which ought to be in all things an example to new Christian communities in distant lands, is rent into hostile sects and parties, each of which is accustomed to look only on " its own things," and too often thinks it serves God by ignoring God's gifts to its neighbours. The missionary spirit, which is the spirit of Christ and of love, has done much to mitigate both the spirit of divisiveness and the spirit of exclu- siveness; but, partly from the resistance which relentless theories offer to charity, and partly from ignorance, few even of the friends of Missions in England seem to have much relish for looking upon " the things of others." In India, and throughout the Mission- field, the missionary spirit has freer scope, and has generally brought about a more satisfactory state of things. The religious divisions which originated in England, and which are fed from England, have not, it is true, been healed in India; but the feelings out of which those divisions arose have been repressed, and care has been taken that they should have as few opportu nities as possible of breaking out into action. The various Missionary Societies, on sending out Missionaries to India, have generally selected, as the sphere of their labours, some extensive district some province or kingdom in which the name of Christ was entirely, or almost entirely, unknown; and in such unoccupied regions they have located their Missionaries, in the hope that they would not be tempted to interfere with tba Mis sionaries of any other Society, and that they would be exemps from the danger of being themselves interfered with. This is the rule which has generally been acted upon in Southern India ; and hence, in most Provinces, Christianity exhibits but one phase. In Malabar and Canara, the only Mission is that of the Lutherans ; in the Cochin and Malayalam-speaking portion of Travancore, that of the Church Missionary Society; in the Tamil portion of Travancore, that of the London Missionary Society ; in Tinne- velly, those of the two Church of England Societies; in the greater part of Madura, that of the American Board of Missions. This is undoubtedly the general rule, and although there are exceptions, the only exception of any importance is that of the Leipsic Society. That Society has intruded into almost every part of the field of labour occupied by the Society for the Propagation of the Gospel in the province of Tanjore, and received with open arms all who have seceded from our congregations on the ground of our discouragement of caste. Were it not for this lamentable exception, it might have been said that the antagonism of rival sects and parties is unknown in the Indian Mission-field, and that though the religious divisions of Europe exist, they have been deprived of their sting. After all, this is an exceptional case, and the general rule is that which I have mentioned.

The Missionaries of the various Societies cannot, it is true, amalgamate ; even cooperation, in the proper sense of the term, is impracticable. But if there is no amalgamation and no coope ration, at any rate, with the solitary exception referred to, there is no antagonism, because there is no proselytism. The rule by which all consent to be bound is that of friendly non-interference; and hence when Missionaries of different communions or of different Societies meet, they meet, not as opponents, but as friends and brethren. Even if it should so happen that they are not endowed with any extra largeness of heart, where Christians of any sort are so few and far between, and where Christianity is wrestling for its very existence with a dominant and hateful heathenism, they feel that they cannot afford to "ignore" one another. In the presence of Nan a Sahib, the difference between an English churchman and an English dissenter shrinks into a microscopic point. So anxious are most Missionaries to avoid the possibility of collision, that where the Missionaries of the Society for the Propagation of the Gospel and those of the American Board of Missions found themselves working in the same neigh bourhood, in the confines of Madura and Tinnelly, where it was impossible to fix a boundary-line, the Missionaries of the former Society proposed, and the Missionaries of both Societies agreed, that neither Society should be at liberty to establish a school or congregation within a mile of any place where the other Society already had either. Such rules and such feelings have their counterpart in every other portion of the Mission-field. I need not remind the readers of the publications of the Society for the Propagation of the Gospel, how entirely they are in agreement with the sentiments and practice of the

South-African Bishops, and the Bishop of New Zealand.

Even in the greater cities of India, where the excellent rule referred to cannot be acted upon, and where the Missionaries of various Societies carry on their work in somewhat of a promis cuous manner, it would be an error to suppose that the conversion of the Hindus to Christ is hindered by the spectacle of a divided, quarrelsome Christianity. Divisions do, it is true, exist, and it is a pity that they do ; but at any rate it is a consolation that they are not apparent to the Hindu".

In everything which, according to Hindu notions, constitutes a religion, in everything in which Christianity differs from Brahmanism, all Protestant Missionaries appear to the Hindus to be at one. When they see that all Missionaries expound and circulate the same sacred volume, translated into the vernacular; that they all preach salvation through the death of the same Divine Saviour; that they all represent faith as the means of obtaining release from sin, and as the seed of virtue; that they are all free from the suspicion of idolatry ; that they all offer to the same God, through the same Mediator, the " reasonable service" of prayers and praises in the vernacular language; when they find also that they are all alike, or as nearly alike as indi vidual peculiarities will permit, in purity and elevation of cha racter ; that they live on terms of friendly intercourse with one another, repudiate mutual proselytism, and evidently rejoice in one another's successes, they cannot but regard them as teachers of one and the same religion, bearing the united testimony of many independent witnesses to the truths which they teach in common. It is also to be borne in mind that Brahmanism is peculiarly tolerant of diversities. The Hindus are accustomed to regard truth, not as one-sided, but as many-sided, and their most popular philosophy represents this as a necessary result of Divine knowledge coming in con tact with the multiplied varieties of human ignorance. It will be considered by some persons a more legiti mate ground of consolation that heathens cannot become acquainted with any matter on which a really serious difference exists amongst Christians until after they have made up their minds to become Christians themselves. The only doctrines which are, or can be, preached to heathens are those on which all Protestant Christians are agreed, and questions respecting the nature and authority of the ministry and the government of the Church necessarily lie over till heathens have been converted and admitted into the Church. I cannot admit that there is any dereliction of principle in volved in the system of mutual forbearance which I have now described. We exemplify our own principles in our own sphere, and teach our own converts our own views: \re merely refrain from unwarranted intermeddling with the labours of others. There is no disposition on the part of the Missionaries of the Church of England to give up or to undervalue the order and the coherence, the strength and the beauty of the organization which has descended to us from primitive times ;

and in this race of systems, v/herever ours should rank, it certainly does not rank hindmost. Everywhere, it is true, more depends upon the man than upon his system. A good, devoted man with a defective system will do more good than a feeble-minded, unearnest man with the best system in the world: but I will say, and I say it without any disparagement of the results which Christians of other commu nions have effected, that where the system of the Church of England is administered by men who are worthy of it, where it is enabled to free itself from the complications and trammels which, like parasitic plants, have twined themselves round it in the course of ages, but which are no part of itself, where it freely' adapts itself to the circumstances of the place, and incor porates into itself all the good it finds there, it is one which cannot easily be matched; and every one who has visited our Missions in Tinnevelly, where this course has generally been followed, will admit, I think, that the condition of those Missions goes far to prove this point.

Though I have represented the progress of Missions in India as, on the whole, encouraging, I trust it will be remembered that what has been done is literally as nothing compared with what remains to be done. If we would fulfil the purposes which Divine Providence appears to have had in view in giving us our Indian empire, we must put forth efforts of a very different order from what we have hitherto done, and especially so now, that we have been roused from our apathy by one of the most terrible visitations with which any nation was ever chastised and warned. I cannot forbear adding, that whilst some other communions are doing more than could reasonably have been expected, and whilst the Missionary Societies of the Church of England have shown their capacity for doing well whatever they are enabled to do, there are multitudes of persons, calling themselves members of the Church of England, who either render those Societies no help whatever in their great work, or mock them with help of the most niggardly kind. If higher and more worthy motives should fail to kindle in the minds of such persons some missionary zeal, I would bring before them, if I could reach their ear, a few facts which might perhaps " provoke them to jealousy."

In 1852, when an analysis of the missionary statistics of India was made, it appeared that the two Societies of the Church of England employed in India and Ceylon 138 Missionaries, or, if we add European Catechists, as was done in the enumeration of the Missionaries of the non-Episcopal Societies, the number may be raised to 160. Now, one of the facts which I should wish " easy-going" churchmen to become acquainted with is, that at the same period the Missionaries of the non-Episcopal societies numbered 30G. Surely the proportion between those numbers is not what it ought to be. In so far as results are concerned, the scale undoubtedly turns more in our favour; for whilst our Missionaries were but 34 per cent, of the entire number, the native converts connected with our Missions amounted to 57 per cent. But though we may hope that God's blessing will continue to rest upon our labours, it is unsatisfactory to find that our labours fall so far short of those of others ; and it may be added, that in the end Providence is generally found to favour most those who labour most. There is an important truth at the bottom of Bonaparte's irreverent saying, " Providence sides with heavy battalions." Another fact, which some persons will be still less prepared to hear, is, that the Americans and the Germans are doing far more for India, proportionately to their interest in it, than is being done by English churchmen. India has been expressly com mitted, by Divine Providence, to the care of England, and England derives from India immense temporal advantages. America has received no special call to evangelize India ; yet the two non-Episcopal Missionary Societies of the United States main tain in India and Ceylon no less than 67 Missionaries. When we compare this number with the 100 Missionaries maintained by the Church Missionary Society, and the 60 maintained by the Society for the Propagation of the Gospel, I think it must be admitted that the comparison, in so far as it is an indication of zeal and enterprise, is not very much in our favour. Is it not well fitted to " provoke us to jealousy," that the Presbyterians and Congregationalists of the United States should feel themselves obliged to send Missionaries to the British possessions in India, to teach Christianity to the subjects of the British crown ?

The zeal of the Germans for the evangelization of India puts us to still greater shame. It is considered as a matter of course that the Germans should know more about the antiquities of India, as of every other country, than we do ; but if so " prac tical " a people as we are should be left behind by the Germans in so practical a work as the propagation of the Gospel in our own territories, it would justly be considered, not as a matter of course, but as a national disgrace.

What, then, are the facts 1 The small and poor Basle Mis sionary Society employs 27 Missionaries in India ; the smaller and poorer Leipsic and Berlin-Gossner Societies, 34 ; and 38 Germans are employed by English Societies, most of them by the Church Missionary Society. Thus, in all 99 Germans are labour ing as Missionaries in India ; and though nearly half of that number are supported by English funds, yet surely to give men, for such a cause, especially such men as many of them are, is a greater proof of interest in it than to give money. Leaving out of account whence their support is derived, leaving also out of account their present ecclesiastical connexion, and looking only at the country where they were born and bred, and where they received their first missionary impulse, I find that there is a larger number of Germans labouring as Missionaries in the British possessions in India than of English-born members of the Church of England. Can any member of the Church of England can any Englishman feel satisfied with this state of things?

It is a token for good that the funds of the Society for the Propagation of the Gospel, as those of her sister, the Church Mis sionary Society, are steadily increasing. Our income for the last year (1856) exceeded that of the previous year by 3,000?., and the previous year's income exceeded that of the one before by 15,0001. It is now possible, therefore, for the Society to do:nore for India. I arn aware that our ever-increasing colonies have the first claim upon its assistance ; but, notwithstanding that admis sion, I greatly regret that the number cf its Missionaries and the amount of its expenditure in India have hitherto borne so very small a proportion to the work which is to be accomplished. Few of our friends are aware how far we have been left behind in the race by other Societies. In 1856, leaving out of account sums raised and expended in India, the Society for the Propagation of the Gospel expended on India Missions 19,000?., of which 2,800?. were absorbed by Bishop's College, Calcutta. This is no doubt, a considerable sum, and it betokens the existence of a considerable degree of interest in the welfare of India ; but it shrinks into less imposing dimensions when compared with the amounts expended by other Societies. Leaving out, as before, sums raised in India, the Church Missionary Society expended during the same period on Indian Missions 44,000?., the London Missionary Society 20,500?., and even the American Board of Missions one of the two American Societies labouring in India 17,000?. May I not reasonably wish that the Society for the Propagation of the Gospel the oldest of all our Societies stood higher in the scale ? The Society would be delighted to have it in its power to expend more ; but it can expend only what it receives. If its friends would open their hearts and hands, and promote its cause with a more affectionate zeal, and if the number of its friends should be increased, we should undoubtedly be enabled to move forward ; but if otherwise, in answer to the cry of India, " Come over, and help us," the Society will be obliged to send out, not Missionaries, but regrets.

I am happy to say that this fear has been dispelled, and that the aid I hoped for has been granted. Within a month after I gave expression in the Colonial Church Chronicle to these regrets and hopes, the Financial Committee of the /Society for the Pro pagation of the Gospel reported upon a plan for the expenditure of the Society's increased income, and an additional grant of 3,000?. a year, for three years, was voted for the extension of Indian Missions. Thus whilst Providence is so loudly calling upon us to go forward, whilst new openings for usefulness are daily pre senting themselves to us, we shall no longer be under the necessity of abandoning our outposts and narrowing the circle of our use fulness, as we had latterly been obliged to do in India, but will be enabled, I trust, to follow whither Providence leads.

I am truly thankful to record this improvement in the Society's position, and I trust that it is not only in itself a considerable step in advance, but a sign and pledge of progressive improve ment. All that has been accomplished as yet may be described as only a promising beginning. More has been done in Tinne- velly than in any other province in India, and yet very much remains to be done before all Tinnevelly is Christianized. 43,000 souls have been brought under Christian instruction in that one province, but more than 1,200,000 souls remain in darkness still ! It is frequently our duty still, in the ordinary course of our labours in Tinnevelly, within the limits even of our Missionary parishes, to pass through village after village, teeming with a busy population, in which all classes of society " old men and maidens, young men and children," vie with each other, not in praising and serving God, but in praising and serving devils. Much remains to be done atao before every Indian province, or even every province in the Madras Presidency, becomes a Tiune- velly ; for, with the exception of the three or four most southern provinces, Southern India has witnessed no greater Missionary progress than the Presidencies of Bengal and Bombay. Even in Southern India I could mention twelve or thirteen Zillahs or provinces, each with an average population of nearly a million of souls, in all which there is not a single Missionary of the Church of England. In most of those provinces there are one or two Missionaries of other societies ; but in the Hyderabad country, which is connected with Madras in ecclesiastical matters, though politically connected with Bengal, and in which there is a popu lation of ten millions, the great majority of them Telugu people and heathens, there is not a single European Missionary connected with any Protestant communion. There is an excellent native Missionary labouring there, a Missionary of the Society for the Propagation of the Gospel ; but lie can scarcely be regarded as a Missionary to the people of the country. Being himself a Tamil man, he was sent on a special mission to the Tamil people who have settled as domestic servants to the Europeans, and as camp followers in the principal military cantonment; yet the appoint ment of that solitary native Missionary is all that has been done for the propagation of Christianity in the territories of the Nizam. To hope to dispel the darkness of ten millions of heathens and Mahometans by an isolated effort like that, is surely little better than if we should hope to illuminate London by means of a single candle stuck upon the top of St. Paul's !

I trust, however, that more will soon be done for India in general, and more also for Tinnevelly, to which my own mind naturally reverts when I think of the future. Supposing the congregations already gathered in in Tinnevelly, able to stand alone without foreign aid, which I hope they will, ere long, be able to do, it will then become only more clearly our duty and a delightful duty it will be to lengthen our cords, and strengthen our stakes, and endeavour to gather in more and more of the surrounding heathenism.

Hinduism, which wears a calm and tolerant face when it fears no danger, has recently shown, by its combination with Mahometan fanaticism, and its ebullitions of persecuting rage, that it feels the grasp, and fears the power and progress of its Divine foe. A crisis now appears in the history of our Missions in India, and surely the appearance of such a crisis should stimulate the friends of Missions, and all who are desirous of the enlightenment and improvement of India, to help us with all their might. The Church Missionary Society has every year of late been devoting more and more of its funds and energies to India ; and now that I am about to return to the scene of my own labours, I am truly thankful to carry with me the hope and belief that the Society for the Propagation of the Gospel has also commenced to move forward. The additional grant which the Society has recently been enabled to make for the extension of Indian Missions, provides us with funds sufficient for a considerable advance in each of the Presidencies ; and now all that we want is an adequate supply of men of the proper sort. " The harvest truly is great, and the labourers are few ; " and without the help of additional labourers, men of piety, de- votedness, and energy, the harvest cannot be gathered in. " Say not ye, There are yet four months, and then cometh harvest Lift up your eyes, and look on the fields ; for they are white already unto harvest. And he that reapeth receiveth wages, and gathereth fruit unto life eternal." The real work of Missions, the work of winning souls to Christ, is a spiritual work, and can only be done by spiritual men. Living men alone are competent to place " living stones " in the wall of the spiritual temple. But such men are not to be purchased by money ; no organization, however perfect no ordination, however valid, can confer life. If we wish Christian men, animated by the living, loving Spirit of Christ, to be raised up and sent forth to do Christ's work in India, such men must be sought for in Christ's Spirit, and in accordance with Christ's commands, by earnest prayers to Himself; for surely He is more deeply interested than we can be in the extension and prosperity of his own work.

"Pray ye, therefore, the Lord of the harvest, that He would thrust forth labourers into his harvest."

LECTURE 1

Tinnevelly is one of those "Collectorates," "Zillahs," or provinces, each comprising about a tenth of the area of England, into which British India is divided, and is the most southerly province on the eastern side of India, or, as it is termed, the Coromandel Coast. Cape Comorin, the southern extremity of the Indian peninsula, is included in the native state of Travancore, on the Malabar or Western Coast; but Tinnevelly may be regarded as commencing at Cape Comorin, for it commences only about three miles to the east of the Cape. It contains an area of 5,482 square miles, and a population of 1,269,216 souls; consequently, the population amounts to 233 in the square mile, which is exactly equal to the average population of the midland counties in England. Tinnevelly is separated from Travancore by the great mountain chain of the Ghauts, which form its western boundary, and on the east it is bounded by the Gulf of Manaar, by which it is separated from Ceylon. Its greatest length to the north-east is about 120 miles, and its greatest breadth from east to west about 75 miles.

The southern extremity of the province being only 8 5' north of the equator, the heat is necessarily very great. During the whole period of my residence in Tinnevelly, I never noticed the thermometer lower than 70, and rarely so low as that. When it sinks to 75 we call it cold weather, and put on additional clothing. Though our so-called cold weather is warmer than the average of summer heat in England, it is a comfort that during the hot season the thermometer is not proportionately high. I have not known it higher in my own house at any period of the year than 91, and it is rarely more than a few degrees higher even in the hottest localities. This would be reckoned a very moderate degree of summer heat in Northern India, where, though it sometimes sinks in the cold weather to the freezing-point, it rises in the hot season to 110 or even 120 in the shade. In Tinnevelly such violent extremes of temperature are unknown, the annual range being rarely more than 20; but owing to the entire absence of cold weather, properly so called, the aggregate of heat throughout the year is much greater than in Northern India. We have not the alternatives of being roasted one part of the year and frozen the other, but gently simmer over a slow fire the whole year round. On the other hand, the heat of Tinnevelly is not a moist, enervating heat, like that of the Malabar Coast and Ceylon, but a dry, healthy heat; and there are few provinces in India which agree so well, on the whole, with the European constitution. As there is no province in India where Missionaries are more numerous, so there is none where they enjoy better health or are able to remain longer in their spheres of duty. Though the dryness of the air may be conducive to the health of the inhabitants, it is far from being conducive to the fertility of the soil. The drought is so excessive, that much of the land lies uncultivated. On the southern coast, where my own residence was, the average annual fall of rain was only 22 inches, which is less than the average fall in England j and three -fourths of the entire quantity fell during a single month, November. Only 35 inches of rain were registered during the three years that elapsed before I left! This excessive drought is owing to the influence of the Ghauts, the great mountain range, or rather mountain-plateau, by which Southern India is divided into two portions, the Coromandel and Malabar coasts. The steep sides of this plateau form a continuous chain of mountains from near Cape Comorin for about 200 miles northwards, and the breadth of the plateau gradually increases from a single rock at the Cape to about 80 miles at "the Coimbatoor gap." The average height of the ridge is about 3,000 feet, but there are peaks which rise to double that height. This elevated range acts as an effectual barrier to the rains of the South- West monsoon, which is the great monsoon, or periodical rainy season, of India, and to which the greater part of India owes its fertility. On the Malabar Coast, the western side of the Ghauts, there is a great abundance of rain: consequently, we have there perpetual verdure, and per petual fertility and beauty ; for in the tropics, wherever we have rain, we have all the elements of vegetable wealth. But on the eastern side of the Ghauts, on the Coromandel Coast, including the whole of the Carnatic, the supply of rain from the South-West monsoon is almost entirely intercepted by the Ghauts: the North- Eastern monsoon, which is the special monsoon of the Coromandel Coast, compensates but partially for the absence of the South- Western ; and the evil reaches its maximum in Tinnevelly, which is not only shut out from the South- West monsoon, but is robbed, by the vicinity of Ceylon, of half its due share of the North-Eastern. Ceylon does not lie wholly to the south of India, as is sometimes supposed ; its northern extremity is nearly two degrees to the north of Cape Comorin, and hence the whole length of Tinnevelly is overlapped by it. Though so little rain falls in Tinnevelly, and though the greater part of the province suffers severely in consequence, there are regions which are as fertile and beautiful as the eye could desire. Besides smaller rivers, there is one of considerable magnitude, and of great celebrity and sacredness, the Tamravarni, or " copper-coloured " river, which irrigates and fertilizes the ex tensive tract of country through which it flows ; and as this river rises in the Ghauts, it is filled by the rains of both monsoons, so that two crops of rice every year are produced all along its banks..Similar advantages are enjoyed by the rich and beautiful districts in the vicinity of the mountains ; and hence, though Tinnevelly does not participate directly in the rains of the South- Western monsoon, yet in the neighbourhood of the rivers and mountains it participates indirectly, yet largely, in the fertilizing influences of those rains. In consequence of this, in the amount of revenue derived from " wet cultivation," that is, rice, andc., Tinnevelly ranks next to Tanjore amongst South-Indian provinces.

Notwithstanding the advantages enjoyed by particular portions of the province, nine-tenths of the entire area are parched and arid through excessive drought, and there are districts as sandy, burnt up, and dreary as any in the deserts of Africa. I have stood on a mountain peak about twenty miles from Cape Comorin, from which both Travancore and Tinnevelly are visible at once, and have been exceedingly struck with the difference ; Travan core beautifully green, and diversified with hill and dale, wood, lake, and river ; Tinnevelly an immense fiery-red plain, with signs of cultivation few and far between. On closer acquaintance, -the reality is found to be better than the appearance ; for the " regur," or blistered "black cotton soil" of the northern dis tricts is well adapted to the growth of cotton, about 60,000 bales of which are annually shipped at Tutocorin for England and China, besides what is retained for use in Tinnevelly itself, and.the adjacent provinces: the red sands also of the South-Eastern districts are admirably suited to the growth of the palmyra palm.

In those districts in which the majority of our Mission Churches are planted, the chief dependence of the people is upon the palmyra, which is to them what rice is in Bengal, or wheat in England the staff of life. During the brief and scanty rains of the North-Eastern monsoon, a crop of pulse and of inferior sorts of grain is raised from the better kinds of soil ; and where water is available for irrigation, the plantain, or banana, is largely and successfully cultivated. Along the lower slopes of the " t6ries," or red sand hills, which form so peculiar a feature of the South- Eastern palmyra districts, the water lies near the surface, and is available for plantain gardens ; and hence each of those slopes is beautified by a belt of the richest, brightest green, which presents a grateful contrast to the uncultivated, naked, fiery-red ridges of the "t6ries." The staple produce, however, of the sandy districts is the palmyra. If one were to judge from abstract probabilities, he might expect to find those districts uninhabited ; but Divine Providence is there as well as here, and it has pleased

Providence to ordain that the palmyra palm should flourish more luxuriantly in those sands than in any other part of the East, and should feed an abundant population with its saccharine sap. The sandy districts in the South-East teem with human life, and it is remark able that it is amongst the inhabitants of those districts that Christianity has made greatest progress. Hitherto, from a variety of causes, Christianity and the palmyra have appeared to flourish together. Where the palmyra abounds, there Christian congrega tions and schools abound also ; and where the palmyra disappears, there the signs of Christian progress are rarely seen.

As the majority of the people who have been converted from heathenism in Tinnevelly, and who form the bulk of our Christian congregations, are cultivators of the palmyra, and as most of my own sphere of labour was included in the palmyra forest, I shall here give my readers a description of that remarkable tree.

The palmyra is one of the least elegant of the family of palms, but is, perhaps, the most useful member of the family. It grows to the height of from GO to 90 feet, almost as straight, though not as smooth, as the mast of a ship. Like other palms, it is totally destitute of branches, but is surmounted by an erect plume of fan-shaped leaves, each of which is so large that it may almost be regarded as a branch. Each leaf is shaped like a fan, not pinnated like that of the coco-nut palm, whence it has received its botanical name of Borassus flaldliformis, or " fan-shaped Borassus."* The leaves are stiffer and much less graceful than the long, drooping leaves of the coco-nut, but of all leaves they are the most ser viceable to man. They are not only used for thatching the houses of the middle and lower classes, but are also used for making mats, baskets, and vessels of almost every description ; and a single leaf folded in a particular manner serves as a bucket for drawing water with. But the leaf of the palmyra is put to a still more remark able use: slips of the young leaf form the ordinary stationery of the Hindus in every part of Southern India. Thus in India the " leaf " on which people write is literally a leaf. Each ray, or vein, of the fan-shaped leaf comprises two long slips, and each of those slips will suffice as writing material for an ordinary letter: a collection of leaves strung together constitutes a book. The leaf requires no smoothing or pressing, or any other process of preparation. Just as it comes from the tree it may be used for writing upon ; and as nearly a hundred such slips are supplied by a single leaf, and as a cart-load of leaves may be had for a few shillings, the Hindus are provided with the cheapest species of stationery in the world. It is written upon with an iron pen, or graver, an instrument with a sharp steel point, with which the penman rapidly graves or scratches the characters ; and though the " olei," or palmyra leaf, is not as durable as parchment, or even as paper, yet I have seen documents written on it which were at least 200 years old.

The palmyra is the only palm-tree of which the wood is of any value, and the rafters and laths made of the palmyra are regarded as the best of their kind ; but the high estimate in which the palmyra is held is chiefly owing to the value of its products as articles of food. The young root is edible, and so is the ripe fruit: neither, however, is of much value ; the unripe fruit is greatly preferable, inasmuch as it contains the purest, most wholesome, and most refreshing vegetable jelly in existence.

"Borassus," the generic name of the palmyra, is one of the names which the Greeks gave to the membrane that envelopes the fruit of the Date palm. In after times it came to be used as the botanical name of that family of palms to which the palmyra belongs.,

These articles sink into insignificance when compared with the saccharine sap or juice of the tree, which is by far its most valuable product. The "patha-mr," or unfermented sap. without any cooking or preparation, is very nourishing: during the period when it flows most abundantly, the poorer classes get visibly sleeker and more comfortable, and you might almost see your face in the skin of the children. Just as it comes from the tree, the sap forms the breakfast of the Shanars and lower castes, who drink it in a cup formed for the occasion of a palmyra leaf. The supply of sap is greatly in excess of what is required for daily use, and most of it is boiled into a hard, black mass, called by the English "jaggery " a kind of coarse sugar-cake, which forms the mid-day meal of the same classes. Their evening meal, the principal meal of all Hindus, which is generally of rice, with some curried addita- ments, is procured by the sale of the superfluous "jaggery." The greater part of what is made is sold, and it always commands a ready sale. Some of it is sent to be refined into white sugar for the European market ; and by varying the process a little, the people themselves make a very good sugar-candy. It is the unfermented juice of the palmyra which is used as food: when allowed to ferment, which it will do before mid-day if left to itself, it is changed into a sweet, intoxicating drink, called " kal," or " toddy." This is the liquid which is generally used in India as yeast for leavening bread, but it is also used by the Pariars and other low- caste Hindus, especially in the vicinity of large towns, for the purpose of intoxication. The Shunars, the cultivators of the tree in the southern provinces, are rarely known to make use of it for this purpose: as a caste, they are strictly temperate, in which respect they differ from all other low-caste tribes, and claim to be ranked with the higher castes. One may travel for miles through the thickest part of the palmyra forest, without meeting with a single tree that is licensed to be used for "toddy." Between Edeyenkoody and Sawyerpuram, a distance of thirty-two miles, which I have very frequently traversed,, and which is thickly planted with palmyras throughout, I have only noticed the existence of one " licensed" tree.

The amount of nourishment which is supplied by the palmyra, without even the trouble of cooking, might be supposed to operate as a premium upon indolence ; but, in reality, we find no premium upon indolence in Tinnevelly, or anywhere else in God's world a hard-working world, in which it has been made necessary for every class of people to eat their bread by the sweat of their brow. The Shanars are as industrious a people as any in India ; and if this were not their character, the provision made for their wants would be unavailable, for though their breakfast is ready cooked for them, it is at the top of the palmyra, and the palmyra is a tall, slim tree, without a single branch ; hence it is necessary for every man to climb for his breakfast before he gets it, and the labour of climbing the palmyra in so hot a climate is one of the hardest and most exhausting species of labour anywhere to be seen.

The sap of the tree cannot be obtained, as from the maple, by tapping the trunk ; it flows only from the spadix, or flower-stalk, at the top of the tree. From amongst the fan-shaped leaves, which form the plumed head of the palmyra, there shoot forth in the season several bunches of flower-stalks ; each flower-stalk branches out into several, and each of those flowering branches, when bruised or sliced, yields drop by drop about a pint a day of sweet juice. A little earthen vessel is attached to each " spadix," or flower-branch, to receive the sap as it drops ; and it is the business of such of the Shanars as are palmyra-climbers to cjimb the tree morning and evening, for the purpose of trimming the "palei," or spadix, and emptying into a sort of pail made of pal myra leaf, which they carry up with them, all the sap that they find collected since their last ascent. The pail is then conveyed to a little boiling-house in the neighbourhood, where the women boil the juice into "jaggery." In the northern part of the Carnatic, the palmyra-climbers make use of a sort of movable girdle, to help them in climbing the tree ; but in Tinnevelly and Travancore, in which palmyra-climbing is much more common, the Shanars make no use of any such artificial assistance. They clasp the tree with joined hands, and support their weight not with the knees (which project from the trcv, and of which they make no use,) but with the soles of the feet, which they bend inwards like the hands, and keep together by the help of a little band, so as to enable them to clasp the tree almost as the hands do, and then they ascend, not by the alternate action of each hand, but by a series of springs, in which both hands move together and both feet follow together, not unlike the action used in swimming. A Shanar will climb a palmyra in this manner almost as rapidly as a man will walk the same length, and most of them are accustomed thus to climb fifty trees twice a-day, or even three times a-day, for eight months in the year. Taking sixty feet as the average height of a palmyra, and the climbing of fifty palmyras twice a-day, as the average work of an able-bodied Shanar, we shall form a clear idea of the amount of his work, if we suppose him, every day for the greater part of every year, to climb a perpendicular pole 3,000 feet in height, and then to descend the same pole the same day, ascending and descending without any apparatus, and supporting the entire weight of his body by his strength of limb alone ! Surely no harder work than this has ever been done in a tropical climate. Though the palmyra may be said to resemble a mast, or pole, it must not be supposed to be as smooth. The bark is rough from the scars of former leaves, and this renders the climbing of the tree less difficult, and also less dangerous, than it would otherwise have been. Accidents rarely occur, except in high winds, or when the tree is slippery through recent rain, and not often even then. I knew of a man who was sitting upon a leaf-stalk at the top of a palmyra in a high wind, when the stalk gave way, and he came down eighty feet to the ground, safely and quietly, sitting on the leaf, which served the purpose of a natural parachute.

No kind of cultivation involves so little trouble or expense as that of the palmyra. The nut has merely to be cast into the sand and loosely covered over, and no further thought or care is necessary till it becomes a tree and begins to bear. The farmer is often relieved even of the trouble of planting by the crows, which leave the nut on the ground after devouring the fruit. Sometimes, for two or three years, no trace of the young palmyra appears above ground: it might be supposed to have perished, but it is busily occupied in working its way downwards in search of water. After about twenty years of neglect, this wonderful tree which the Hindus praise as the model of the highest sort of generosity begins to requite its owner for benefits which it never received.

It is remarkable that the palmyra yields its sweet juice not during, or at the close of, the rainy season, when it might be expected to be full of sap, but during the hottest period of the year. The sap begins to rise when the sun returns from the south, and flows most copiously when the sun is righb overhead. The sun is vertical in Tinnevelly in April, and again in August; and the intervening period including also March and Sep tember is what is called the palmyra season. When the heat is BO great and so continuous that every blade of grass disappears from the parched soil when the air is filled with clouds of red sand, hurled along by the land-wind, or South-West monsoon, which mocks with showers of sand the earth's desire for rain then it is that the palmyra yields the abundance of its cool, sweet, refreshing sap, for the supply of the wants of the people. I have dug down through the sandy soil to see where this copious supply of sap came from, and have found the long, stringy roots of the palmyra penetrating right down to a depth of forty feet beneath the surface. There I found them drinking in perpetual draughts of water in the secret springs and channels that lie far beneath the surface of the ground, where the greatest droughts never reach. Even at that depth, I found that they penetrated still lower into interstices amongst the rocks, where I could follow them no longer. Here, then, I found the reason why the palmyra flourishes so well in the sands of

Tinnevelly why it flourishes best where the soil is loosest and sandiest, and why in the hottest season of the year it pours forth from its head such a constant supply of cool, sweet moisture. What a remarkable illustration is this of the wisdom with which Divine Providence makes the peculiarities of every part of the world minister, in some way or another, to the support and advantage of mankind !

Most of the Christian converts in Tinnevelly being Shanar?, and either owners or climbers of the palmyra, at the commence ment of the climbing season I was accustomed to assemble our people in church for a special service, including prayers that the tree might yield its fruit, and that the climber's " foot might not slide;" and on such occasions I have sometimes reminded the people of an appropriate expression in our Tamil version of the psalms Nitima'n panei-pol serippan, " the righteous shall flourish like the palmyra," (the Tamil rendering of Ps. xcii. 11, "the righteous shall flourish like the palm-tree," the palmyra being adopted as the representative of palms in general): and I have then reminded my Shanar hearers, that " the righteous," for this reason amongst others, may be said to " flourish like the palmyra," because he, too, strikes his roots deep beneath the surface the root of faith shoots deep down into the love of God, and "the supply of the Spirit of Jesus Christ;" and hence the righteous " flourishes like the palmyra " in a dry and thirsty land flourishes most not in the richest soil, but in the poorest, in afflictions and persecutions, and is continually bringing forth fruit for the refreshment of mankind. Thus, in Tinnevelly, as everywhere else in the world, there are " sermons " in trees and stones, "and good in everything." Our attention must now be turned from the country to the people.

In consequence of Tinnevelly lying at the southern extremity of the Indian peninsula, there are few provinces in India in which ancient Hindu usages have been so faithfully preserved. Five hundred years had elapsed from the time of the arrival of the Mahometans in India, before the wave of Mahometan conquest reached and overspread Tinnevelly j and hence the Mahometans are fewer and less influential here than elsewhere. The language of the province is Tamil, and the Tamil spoken by the educated classes in Tinnevelly is singularly pure and classical. Even amongst the lower classes, notwithstanding their rude pro nunciation, the language of the ancient poets still lingers. The Tamravarni, or Palamcottah river, is represented by native writers as the southern boundary of the Sen-Tamir nadu, or " Classical-Tamil country," and the -whole of the province, together with the southern districts of Travancore, was included in the ancient Pandiyan empire an empire of which Madura was the capital city, and which sent two embassies to the Emperor Augustus.

The inhabitants of Tinnevelly, as of most other provinces in India, may be divided into the three classes of Brahmans, Sudras, and lower classes; and, as elsewhere, it is chiefly amongst the lower classes that Christianity has made progress.

The Brahmans spring from a different origin from the rest of the Hindus, and claim kindred with ourselves. They are the lineal representatives of that Sanscrit-speaking race, allied to the Greeks and Germans, which conquered the Punjab at least 1500 years before the Christian era, and which rendered ancient India so illustrious for philosophy, literature, and the cultivation of the arts. Tinnevelly, like every other part of India, owes its higher civilization to the Brahmans, who appear to have formed colonies along the fertile banks of the Tamravarni six or seven centuries before the Christian era, and gradually made themselves revered by the aboriginal tribes as their guides, philosophers, and friends. They founded amongst the Dravidians, or South-Indians, a succession of civil communities modelled after the empires of Northern India, and taught the rude chieftains of the South to imitate the cultivated tastes of the " Solar " and "Lunar" dynasties. Notwithstanding the value of these services to society, it is questionable whether they are not outweighed by the evils which the Brahmans introduced idol worship, a routine of inane ceremonies, morbid scrupulosity respecting meats and drinks, an unpractical philosophy, and the division and subdivision of the people into castes. The Brahmans have become much more numerous than in the olden time, but much less influ ential. They still, it is true, rank at the head of native society as a sacred, priestly aristocracy, which has not degraded itself by a single intermarriage with the classes beneath it for 2,500 years; but individually the Brdhmans have now little religious or social influence beyond what they possess as respectable landed pro prietors. The greater number even of the priestly functions, except in the more important temples, are now performed in Southern India by Sudras, who form, undoubtedly, the most influ ential portion of the community; and though they are rarely more willing than the Brahmans to embrace Christianity, they seldom evince that, scorn of it, as a foreign or low-caste religion, which the Brahmans generally evince. So far as I am aware, only one Tinnevelly Brahman has, as yet, become a Christian.

The un-Brahmanical, or aboriginal Hindus, who are ordinarily styled " the Tamil people," " the Telugu people," andc., and who constitute nine-tenths of the population everywhere in Southern India, belong not to the Aryan or Indo- Germanic, but to the Turanian or Scythian race that race to which the Mongols, the Turks, and the Finns belong ; and the vernacular languages of Southern India, though occupying a distinct position of their own amongst the various families of human speech, have a greater resem- Hance to the Finnish tongues than to any other class. The South Indian aborigines, having received from the Brahmans the elements of their higher civilization, were divided by their Brahman in structors into castes, and have become as zealous for caste as the Brahmans themselves. All the castes into which they were divided maybe classified into two easily recognized divisions ; viz. the higher or Sudra group, including the " cultivators," merchants, artificers, shepherds, andc. ; and the lower castes, beginning with the Shanars, including the Pariars, and other agricultural slaves, and ending with the wandering gipsy tribes. I regard the lower castes not as the descendants of a race of aborigines still older than the Tamilians, but as the descendants of those Tamilians who happened to occupy a low position in the social scale, as servants or slaves, at the period when the Brahmanical caste system was introduced, and who have been prevented by that fossilizing system from ever emerging from the position they then occupied. The Siidra castes of Southern India occupy a position in society much superior to that of the Sudras in the North. The castes called by that name in the North belong to the lower classes: the Sudras of the South answer closely to our "middle classes;" they form the staple of population in the towns and in the richer country districts; manufactures, commerce, the administration of justice and education, are mainly in their hands, and it is to them that the people of the lower castes generally look as their natural heads and guides.

A considerable proportion of the Tinnevelly Sudras in some districts a large majority of them have sprung from a Telugu origin, and speak Telugu in their own homes, though they com municate with their neighbours freely enough in Tamil. They belong to the Telugu castes of Reddies, Naiks, andc., and are descendants of those men at arms and adventurers who followed the fortunes of the Vijaya-nagar generals, by whom the Chola and Pandiya dynasties were subverted in the fifteenth century, and who were rewarded for their services by donations of uncul tivated lands in various districts, especially in the northern part of Tinnevelly. These Telugu castes rank lower than the corre sponding Tamil castes in point of social respectability, but in domestic morals they rank lower still. The married life of the middle classes of the Tamil people is singularly free from blame ; but all sorts of irregularities and abominations prevail amongst the Telugu settlers, and instead of exposing the guilty parties to disgrace, are sanctioned by the law of the caste. Hence, in addition to the ordinary difficulties in the way of the reception of Christianity by persons of caste, the Reddies are deterred from it (and sometimes, after they hate nominally received it, are induced to abandon it) by its pure morality. It was from this cause, amongst others, that the promising movement amongst the Reddies in the north of Tinnevelly, of which so much was heard seven or eight years ago, came to nothing. Though the pure Tamil castes present a favourable contrast to the Telugu settlers in point of domestic morals, they are con sidered to be, and probably are, more untruthful and slippery. They are commonly regarded as the least scrupulous and as the most adventurous of Hindu races. One can hardly fail to read n their very look the habit of gaining their purpose by a circuitous path, and of overcoming opposition not by open resistance, but by a feigned, temporary compliance.

No Indian people, not even, I think, the Brahmans, have reached a higher point of civilization than the Tamilian Siidras ; but their civilization, like that of every Asiatic people, is partial and unequal. One meets with as many degrees of civilization as of complexion. Stupendous hewn-stone temples and mean mud- built habitations, a scrupulous regard for ceremonial purity, and a shameful disregard of decency and drains, institutions of con summate policy and follies of which sensible children would be ashamed, exist everywhere side by side. Indian civilization is full of inconsistencies and incongruities: it is lacking in expan- siveness and in progress ; but its most grievous defect consists in the absence of that scorn of lies and that keen sense of honour which are inherent in Christian civilization, and which charac terize the Christian gentleman.

Notwithstanding the high civilization which the high-caste Hindus, and especially the Tamilians, have reached, and their fondness for religious speculation and ceremonial, they are deeply sunk in spiritual ignorance and mental torpor. In no country in the world does religion enter so largely into the affairs of life and the usages of society as in India: it pervades the entire frame work of society, and mixes itself up in every concern, whether public or private, in which the people are interested ; and yet in no country has religion exerted so little influence for good. There are ancient sects and modern sects, austere sects and licentious sects, high-soaring metaphysical sects and grovelling materialist sects, sects that worship the gods and sects that worship the demons, sects that worship the sun and sects that worship the snake, sects that worship everything and sects that worship nothing ; but the results of each and all seem exactly iden tical they leave men where they found them, or make them worse. They are reckoned by the Brahmans themselves as equally useful, which means, I presume, that they are equally useless.

It used to be said by the Duke of Wellington, that " education without religion made people clever devils: " recent events in India prove that this may be said with still greater truth of the effects of civilization without religion, or, what is still worse, if possible, civilization with a bad religion. The tiger's step becomes softer and its coat sleeker, but it remains as much of a tiger as ever. Human nature when left to itself is bad enough, but it becomes still worse when the devil, in the shape of a bad religion, gets the management of it, and when God's gifts are placed at the devil's disposal.

I may here remark, that it is the peculiar policy of the Brahmans to render all the religious systems of India subservient to their purpose by making friends of them all. Brahmanism repudiates exclusiveness ; it incorporates all creeds, assimilates all, consecrates all. People are permitted to entertain any opinions they please, and to practise any ceremonies they please, provided only that the supremacy of the Vedas and of the Brahmans is acknowledged. When that acknowledgment has been duly made, the new heterodoxy becomes another new authoritative orthodoxy, especially revealed by the Supreme Being himself for the enlightenment and salvation of the parti cular class of people amongst whom it has become popular. Thus Brahmanism yields and conquers ; and hence, though the demon-worship of Tinnevelly is as far as possible repugnant to the genius of orthodox Hinduism, and was not only independent of it in origin, but, as I believe, long anterior to it, yet even it has received a place in the cunningly-devised mosaic of the Brahmans, and the devils have got themselves regarded as abnormal developments of the gods.

It is one of the peculiar difficulties that Christianity has to encounter in dealing with Hindus of the higher and middle castes, that the religion of the country is so closely intertwined with the usages of Hindu society. The more punctilious a high-caste Hindu is in the performance of his religious ceremonies, and in the maintenance of his caste purity and exclusiveness, the higher are supposed to be his claims to social respectability. It is not necessary for him to be a believer in the doctrines of his religien; but it is absolutely necessary, if he is a man of " good caste" and in affluent circumstances, that he should carefully practise all its rites. He cannot keep his place in society, he cannot claim to be regarded as a gentleman, without affecting to be superstitious. A poor low-caste man may be as careless as he likes about his religious duties ; but one who occupies a respectable position in society cannot choose but show himself ceremonious, just as an English gentleman cannot choose but live in a style appropriate to his rank. Hence, to propose to a Hindu of respectability to abandon all the usages of his sect and caste, and embrace a foreign religion, sounds in his ear like asking him to abandon the pro prieties of life and become a Pariar. No class of people are so enslaved to custom and precedent as those who are wealthy and luxurious without being enlightened.

Another difficulty in the way of the spread of the Gospel amongst that class is owing to the tyranny of caste. A caste man may, indeed, become a Christian after a fashion without giving up his caste, though he cannot become a Christian without ceasing to be respectable ; but if he should be so thoroughly con vinced of the truth of Christianity, and so completely disen thralled by it, as to determine to give up not only his false creed, but his caste exclusiveness, he must be content to suffer not only the loss of social status, but the loss of everything which life holds dear. The government, indeed, will protect his person and his life; it has recently guaranteed to him also his right to his paternal inheritance, and so far his condition is better than that of converts to Christianity under the Roman Emperors ; but the Government cannot protect him from being abandoned by his relations, excluded for ever from the society of his equals, and condemned to life-long reproach and disgrace.

"W hat to require of a caste man on his becoming a Christian, is a perplexed question involved in many difficulties. If he is required, as he now generally is, to give up caste at once and submit to social excommunication, other persons similarly situated are deterred from following his example, notwithstanding their conviction of the truth of Christianity, and thus the narrow entrance to the way of life is made narrower: if, on the other hand, he is received into the Church without giving up caste, in the expectation that this part of his duty as a Christian will be fulfilled at some future period, when he has obtained more light and strength, it is found that the caste usages and unsocial dis tinctions that have been retained the Canaanites that have been spared in the land wax stronger, instead of weaker, every year, and at length begin to pave the way for the re-introduction of heathenism.

Amongst the Sudra or middle-class portion of the population of Tinnevelly, Christianity has made, as yet, but little progress. Of the 43,000 converts who are registered in our church-lists, not more than a thousand are members of that class, "and the majority of that thousand belong to the lowest division of it. The Sudra inhabitants of Tinnevelly have not embraced Christianity more generally, or shown themselves better disposed towards it, than persons belonging to similar castes in other provinces. On the contrary, much greater progress was made amongst persons of this class in Tanjore by Swartz and his immediate successors. It is amongst the Shandna'rs, or palmyra cultivators, a caste which is almost restricted to Tinnevelly and South Travancore, that Christianity has made most progress ; and though the movement has extended to some other castes, higher and lower in the social scale, almost all the missionary results for which Tinnevelly is famous have been accomplished amongst the Shanars. Shana"r Christianity still forms the staple of the Christianity of Tinnevelly.

In some respects the position of the Shanars in the scale of castes is peculiar. Their abstinence from spirituous liquors and from beef, and the circumstance that their widows are not allowed to marry again, connect them with the Sudra group of castes. On the other hand, they are]not allowed, as allSudras are, to enter the temples ; and where old native usages still prevail, they are not allowed even to enter the courts of justice, but are obliged to offer their prayers to the gods and their complaints to the magistrates outside, and their women, like those of the castes still lower, are obliged to go uncovered from the waist upwards. These circum stances connect them with the group of castes inferior to the Sudras ; but if they musfc be classed with that group, they are undoubtedly to be regarded as forming the highest division of it. A considerable proportion of the Shanars are owners of the land they cultivate, many are engaged in trade, and some of both those classes are wealthy. as wealth is estimated amongst peasantry ; whilst one family, being Zemindars, is entitled to be classed with the gentry of the province. All of them are, in some shape or another, engaged in the cultivation of the palmyra, and perhaps the majority are employed in climbing that tree. Though the Shandnandrs rank as a caste with the lower classes, and though the greater number of them earn their daily bread by their daily labour, pauperism is almost unknown amongst them. Of the great majority it may be said, that they are equally removed from the temptations of poverty and riches, equally removed from the superficial polish and subtle rationalism of the higher castes, and from the filthy habits and almost hopeless degradation of the agricultural slaves. Few of them before their conversion to Christianity are found to be able to read ; and as they form almost the entire population in those districts in which they reside, with little or no opportunity of intercourse with the better-educated classes, their reception of the Gospel is, in most instances, the commencement not only of their spiritual life, but of their intellectual cultivation. Christianity generally finds their minds undeveloped and their manners almost as rude as their ideas, but it does not leave them in the condition in which it finds them. It is the glory of the Gospel that it elevates the social, mental, and moral condition of every people by whom it is embraced, and as the Shanars are by no means deficient in prac tical shrewdness, and are peculiarly willing to be taught, guided, and modelled by those in whom they confide, when once they are induced to embrace Christianity with a sincere faith, the progress they make is peculiarly steady and satisfactory.

In many respects their character is as peculiar as their social position. They are peculiarly docile and tractable, peculiarly fitted to appreciate the advantages of sympathy, guidance, and protection, and peculiarly accessible to Christian influences. Though inferior to many of their neighbours in intellectual attainments, they are by no means inferior to them in sincerity. Their chief faults dissimulation, litigiousness, and avarice are the faults of all Hindus ; but with respect, at least, to dissimula tion, the first and worst of those faults, experience testifies that of all Hindus they are the least guilty. The strong points of the Hindu character are patience, good humour, and natural courtesy, and in these particulars the Shanars are quite on a level with the rest of the Hindus. Less polished than their neighbours, they are not less courteous ; less lively, they are not less good- humoured ; and as for patience, they have been so oppressed and Harassed ever since they were a people, that it is too frequently taken for granted that their patience has no limits. Hence if. their position in the scale of intellect and attainment must be admitted to be low, perhaps no caste of Hindus occupies, as a caste, a more respectable position as regards the moral elements of character. They are a timid people, much exposed to the rapacity of their high-caste neighbours and landlords, and greatly wanting in self-reliance. Accustomed to be led, they are re luctant to be left to themselves, and reluctant to take any step alone. Very sensitive and touchy with respect to the honour due to their caste, that is, to their combined personality, they are apt to resort to combinations for the purpose of gaining caste- privileges, or revenging caste-injuries ; and though individually they are easily influenced, there are no combinations more diffi cult to break or more impracticable than theirs. However convinced of the truth of Christianity they may be, they can rarely be persuaded to act upon their own convictions indepen dently of the course of conduct adopted by their neighbours. They prefer to wait till a party has been formed, and if the party becomes tolerably strong, it then not only dares to act for itself, but often brings with it the entire village community. When a movement of this sort is in progress, nobody likes to anticipate his neighbours, and nobody likes to be left behind.

Most of the peculiarities of the social condition and character of the Shanars, which have now been mentioned, have worked together for their good, and have contributed either to the recep tion of Christianity by members of this caste, or to their growth, in Christian propriety and order after their reception of it. Obstacles which exist elsewhere have no place amongst them, and facilities abound amongst them which are rarely met with else where. We learn from the parable of the Sower, that the different results which attended the preaching of the Gospel in different places were owing, not to the seed, for the seed was in every instance the same, the good seed of the Word, nor to the sower, for the sower was the Lord Jesus Himself, but to differ ences in the soil. Now, amongst the Shanars of Tinnevelly we have the advantage of having a good soil to labour in. In this instance, as amongst the Karens of Burmah, the seed sown amongst a peculiar class of people has brought forth [fruit in peculiar abundance. God's providence may here be observed making straight in the desert a highway for His Gospel, making ready a people " prepared for the Lord," prepared to appreciate Christian teaching and guidance, and prepared to profit by Christian discipline.

The chief peculiarity in the social condition of the Shanars prior to their reception of Christianity was the prevalence amongst them of demonolatry, or the worship of evil spirits. The popular superstitions of the Hindus may be divided into two classes ; viz., the higher or more classical Hinduism, consisting in the worship of the gods and goddesses, heroes and heroines of the Brah- manical Pantheon, and the lower or pre-Brahmanical superstition, deriving its origin from the early inhabitants of India, and con sisting in the worship of devils. A similar demonolatry prevailed amongst the Mongols before their conversion to Buddhism, and amongst the Turks before their conversion to Mahometanism, and survives up to the present day amongst the Ostiaka and other heathen tribes in Siberia. In India, demonolatry is the religion of most of the rude inhabitants of the mountains and pestilential jungles ; and in the provinces in the extreme south, which are farthest removed from the original centres of Brahmanical influence, it prevails even amongst the civilized and partially Brahmanized peasantry. Nowhere does it prevail to a greater extent than in Tinnevelly, where it constitutes the religion of the Shanars and of the whole of the lower classes, and enters very largely into the religion of the middle classes. It was from Tinnevelly or the neighbour hood that demonolatry passed over into Ceylon, where it is mixed up with the Buddhism of the Singhalese. Amongst the middle classes in Tinnevelly demonolatry has received a Brahmanical shape, and pretends to be the worship not of the enemies of the gods, but of sanguinary emanations and energies of the supreme divinities ; but amongst the lower classes it wears no such screen and puts forth no plausible explanations it presents itself as devil-worship " pure and simple." It is true that even the lower classes offer a little passing reverence to the ordinary deities of the country, especially to Subrahmanya, a son of Siva, who has from a very ancient period been the favourite deity of Tinnevelly; but the only worship which they form into a system, the only system which can be styled their religion, the only religion, which has any real hold of their minds, is demonolatry.

The essential features of the demonolatry of Siberia, commonly called Shamanism, and of the demonolatry of Tinnevelly, are identical. Neither system knows anything of a regular priest hood. Ordinarily the head of the family, or the head man of the community, performs the priestly office ; but any worshipper, male or female, who feels disposed, may volunteer to officiate, and the office may at any time be laid aside. Neither amongst the Shamanites, nor amongst the demonolaters of India, is there any belief in the transmigration of souls. Both systems acknowledge in vague terms the existence of a Supreme God ; but they agree in the notion that, if He does exist, He is too good to do people harm, and it is therefore unnecessary to offer Him any kind of worship. The objects of worship in both systems are neither gods nor heroes, but demons, which are supposed to have got the actual administration of the affairs of the world into their hands ; and those demons are so numerous and cunning, so capricious and malicious and powerful, that it is necessary to worship them very sedulously to keep them from doing people mischief.

In Tinnevelly, as in Siberia, bloody sacrifices are offered to appease the anger of the demons ; but the most important and essential feature in the worship of all demonolaters is " the devil- dance." The officiating priest, or " devil- dancer," who wishes to represent the demon, sings and dances himself into a state of wild frenzy, and leads the people to suppose that the demon they are worshipping has taken possession of him ; after which he communicates, to those who consult him, the information he has received. The fanatical excitement which the devil-dance awakens constitutes the chief strength and charm of the system, and is peculiarly attractive to the dull perceptions of illiterate, half- civilized tribes. The votaries of this system are the most sincerely superstitious people in India. There is much ceremony, but little sincerity, in the more plausible religion of the higher classes ; but the demonolaters literally " believe and tremble." In times of sickness, especially during the prevalence of cholera, it is astonishing with what eagerness, earnestness, and anxiety the lower classes worship their demons.

It might naturally be supposed that a pure and spiritual religion, like Christianity, would make little progress amongst a people who are so besotted as to worship devils ; yet in Tinne velly and the neighbouring provinces it has made greater pro gress amongst demonolaters than amongst the followers of the higher Hinduism. The exceeding greatness of the contrast between the fear and gloom of devil-worship and the light and love of the Gospel is found to attract their attention, and it is generally found to be easy to convince them of the debasing character of their own superstition, and of the great superiority of Christianity. We have gone amongst those poor demonolaters as preachers of a religion of mercy, as preachers of " peace on earth and good will to men," and have endeavoured to illustrate its beneficent tendencies by doing them all the good in our power, and especially such good as they could appreciate. We have assured them that God has not abandoned the world He made, but rules it Himself, and is as merciful as He is powerful ; we have given them this convincing proof of His mercy, that " He so loved the world that He gave His only-begotten Son, that whosoever believeth in Him should not perish, but have everlasting life:" we have told them also that it is unnecessary, as well as wrong, to worship devils, through any fear of their malice ; for the Son of God was "manifested" for this very pur pose, " that He might destroy the works of the devil" " by dying He destroyed him that had the power of death, that is, the devil, and delivered those who through fear of death were all their life- time subject to bondage;" so that if they only put their trust in Him, and feared and served Him, he would defend them from all that devils can do. And when they have been induced to listen to these statements and to ponder them in their minds, it has generally been found that of all heathens in India, they are the most ready to throw off the shackles of their slavish fear, and to enter into the enjoyment of the liberty of the children of God. Thus the progress of the Gospel in Tinnevelly has supplied us with another illustration of the truth, that " where sin abounded, grace did much more abound." In a province where devils were literally the objects of worship " where Satan's seat was" the Church of God has received larger accessions of converts than in any other province in India. In Tinuevelly the Church " flourishes like the palmyra" flourishes where perpetual barrenness might have been expected to reign. Hay I not also say that the position which the Shnrs have acquired in the fore-front of Hindu Christianity, notwithstanding their poverty, their want of mental culture, and their lowly rank as a caste, fulfils the prediction, that " there are last which shall be first?"

LECTURE 2

The first attempt to introduce Protestant Christianity into Tinnevelly was made, towards the close of the last century, by the venerable Swartz, who visited the province thrice, and suc ceeded in establishing a congregation of native converts in the fort of Palamcottah. The work which Swartz commenced was efficiently carried on by Jaenicke, another Missionary of the Society for Promoting Christian Knowledge, who was sent to Tinnevelly by Swartz, and who, during the short period in which he retained his health, made Christianity widely known amongst the rural population, and succeeded in planting Christian congregations in several villages in the interior.

With a species of prophetic insight into the future, founded on his observations of the character of the people of the province, and especially of the docility and tractable temper of the con verts, Jaenicke observed, that " there was every reason to hope that at a future period Christianity would prevail in the Tinne velly country." Jaenicke was assisted in his labours by a native Catechist from Tanjore, called Satyanaden, who was ordained in the Lutheran manner by Swartz, and commissioned to carry on in Tinnevelly the promising work which Jaenicke had begun. Satyanaden's labours were eminently successful. It was by him that the members of the Shandnar caste, who still form the bulk of the congregations in almost every part of Tinnevelly, were first reached and influenced ; by him the first Shnar congregation was formed, and the first village of Christian Shanars organized ; and it was in his time that the first of those popular movements originated, which have often since characterized the progress of Tinnevelly Christianity. Satyanaden's first Shanar converts formed themselves for mutual protection into a distinct community, and founded in the heart of the palmyra forest a new village, which they called Mudal-ur, or " Firsttown," a place which subse quently became a sort of metropolis of Shnar Christianity, and formed, during the dark age of the Tinnevelly Missions, a strong hold, to which the persecuted of every caste resorted for protection. Satyanaden's labours in Tinnevelly, though fraught with the promise of abundant fruit, were not long continued, and after his return to Tanjore the new Mission was lamentably neglected. It was visited once by Gericke, in the course of a long missionary tour through the greater part of the Presidency of Madras, and once by Kohlhoff, Swartz's successor in Tanjore. At Kohlhoffs request, Ringeltaube, the founder of the London Missionary Society's Missions in Travancore, bestowed on the Tinnevelly Mission a general oversight for a short period. This expedient was disapproved of by the Christian Knowledge Society, and was discontinued ; but no other European Missionary was sent to occupy the important post which Jaenicke had left vacant, and it is questionable whether the " country priests," or native min isters, who were ordained in Tanjore and sent from time to time to Tinnevelly, did more good or harm, in the absence of European supervision. In 1815, Mr, Hough, then Chaplain to the East India Com pany at Palamcottah, visited the congregations formed by Jaenicke and Satyanfiden, and wrote to the parent Society an interest ing account of the Christian order, steadfastness, and prosperity by which he found them to be characterized. For several j'ears he urged upon the Society the duty of cultivating the promising field to which he had drawn their attention, and especially of sending out a Missionary ; but being disappointed in his endea vours, and a German Missionary, who had been sent out from home, being prevented by sickness from reaching his destination, he asked and obtained from the Church Missionary Society, which had recently commenced to labour in India, the means of esta blishing schools, employing native Catechists, and laying the foundation of a new Mission. Neither would the Church Mis sionary Society have considered it its duty to establish itself in Tinnevelly, nor the London Missionary Society in the adjacent province of Travancore, had it not been for the inability of the older Society, the Society for Promoting Christian Knowledge, to cultivate efficiently those fields of labour, each of which was first offered to that Society by Divine Providence. In 1820, Rhe- nius, one of the ablest, most clear-sighted and practical, and most zealous Missionaries that India has ever seen, was sent by the Church Missionary Society to carry on the Mission which Hough had recently founded, and ere long his energetic labours produced abundant fruit. The old Mission also was placed under his general superintendence ; but the new Mission far outstripped the old ; and at the close of Rhenius's connexion with the Church Missionary Society, after sixteen years of labour, the number of souls rescued by him from heathenism (or by the various agencies set on foot by him), and enrolled under his pastoral care, amounted to more than ten thousand.

Though Rhenius was by birth and education a Lutheran, the views of Church government and worship which he adopted were in general those of the English Dissenters; in consequence of which, some years before his death, his connexion with the Church Missionary Society was dissolved, and it became necessary to reorganize the Mission he founded in some important particulars. Notwithstanding this, his system of working was, as a whole, greatly superior to that of the older Missionaries, Swartz himself not excepted ; and the Tinnevelly Missions are, in a great measure, indebted to him for the progressive element apparent in their history. He was, so far as I am aware, the first Missionary con nected with Church of England Missions in India, by whom caste was in any degree practically repressed, female education syste matically promoted, or societies established amongst native Chris tians for religious and charitable purposes. It is also remarkable that the practice of assembling the people of every Christian village morning and evening for united prayer in church a practice which universally prevails in the missionary congre gations of the Church of England in Tinnevelly, and which has now extended itself to Tanjore and other localities was first introduced by Rhenius.

It was not until after Rhenius's labours and successes had awakened general attention in England, that the Society for the Propagation of the Gospel, (which had inherited the Indian Missions of the Christian Knowledge Society, and which about that time began to participate in the missionary zeal of the present century,) bethought itself of its Missions in Tinnevelly, and resolved to attempt to revive and strengthen them, if they were still found to exist. From 1792 till 1835, those Missions had remained as sheep without a shepherd. The only superintendence of any real value which they had received, had been bestowed upon them by Missionaries of other Societies or by Government Chaplains; and they had passed through seasons of great trial. In 1811, a pestilence swept away in many places a sixth of the community, and about that time many of the Shanar Christians, especially in that part of Tinnevelly which now constitutes my own district, fell back, through fear, to their ancient heathenism. Many persons would suppose that a com munity of Hindu Christians, like that which had been planted in Tinnevelly poor, undisciplined, uneducated, left to itself, sur rounded by heathen influences would soon have ceased to exist. On the contrary, in 1835, when the first Missionary of the Society for the Propagation of the Gospel reached Tinnevelly, and began to inquire about the sheep that had been left to their fate in the wilderness, more than three thousand persons were found to have steadfastly retained the profession of Christianity, and the rites of Christian worship, through an entire generation of neglect. The first two Missionaries, both Germans, who were sent into Tinnevelly by the Society for the Propagation of the Gospel, laboured there for a short period only j their place, however, was immediately supplied by others. Other missionary labourers followed from year to year ; for the Church at home had awoke, the Society for the Propagation of the Gospel had awoke, the Madras Diocesan Committee of that Society had awoke ; and when I now look around in Tinnevelly, instead of the two districts that existed when I arrived, I am rejoiced to see seven, in addition to a new Mission in the Riimnandd country, each of which is provided not only with pastoral superintendence, but also, in a greater or less degree, with the means of extension and advancement. The Church Missionary Society also has continually been lengthening its cords and strengthening its stakes, so that it has now thirteen or fourteen missionary districts, where it only had six when I arrived, and has established besides an organized system of missionary itineration in the northern and less Christianized part of the province.

The Society for the Propagation of the Gospel has reason to be thankful that its ancient Mission in Tinnevelly was found to be capable of revival ; for the revival of an old, neglected Mission is in some respects more difficult than the establishment of a new one. Some of the evils, however, of foregone neglect have clung to the revived Mission; and another consequence is that, as the Church Missionary Society has obtained possession of the greater part of the field, the labours of the older Society are now confined within a very limited compass. When I arrived in Tinuevelly, the spheres of labour of the two Societies had not been defined by territorial boundaries; but it was felt to be desirable that each Missionary should have a district, or missionary parish, of man ageable extent to labour in, that so the possibility of collision, or of mutual interference, might be precluded, and ere long an arrangement of this nature was carried into effect. The field of labour was divided in a fair and friendly spirit, with regard to the actual progress each Society had made; but the consequence is, that the proportion of the area of the province which has fallen to the share of the Society for the Propagation of the Gospel, and for the cultivation of which in future it alone is responsible, amounts now to less than two-fifths of the whole. Notwith standing this restriction within narrower limits, the introduction of the parochial system, with its peaceful adjustment of rights, and its definite apportionment of duties and responsibilities, has, I believe, been attended with the greatest advantages to each Society and to the common cause; and, on looking back upon the past, I attribute to this arrangement a considerable proportion of the prosperity, as well as of the harmony, by which the Missions have been characterized. In the warfare which each Missionary is appointed to carry on, he is now provided with a basis of operations a centre from which Christian influences may radiate. His labours, cares, and responsibilities, being defined by territorial boundaries, he is not so liable, as he otherwise would be, to become disheartened by the vastness of his work, and perplexed by the multiplicity of his cares. The exertions which, if scattered broadcast over the surface of a province, would probably end in failure and disappointment, are confined within moderate and practicable limits. The Missionary is able not only to preach the Gospel again and again in the same village, and to instruct the people systematically in the knowledge of God's word, but also to commend to their reception the religion he teaches by his personal influence, and to watch over and water the good seed which he has sown.

I shall here give a general idea of the results that have been accomplished in Tinnevelly, without some acquaintance with which a description of the work would be comparatively uninteresting ; and in doing so, I make use of the latest statistics that I have been able to obtain.

1. The province has been divided into twenty districts, or mis sionary parishes, each with its parochial organization, and each under pastoral care. 2. Christian congregations have been formed in 684 villages, besides a still larger number of villages that are regularly visited by Missionaries or native teachers. 3. Forty-three thousand souls have been induced to abandon their idols, or their devils, and to place themselves under Christian instruction, of whom 27,000 have been baptized. 4. The number of communicants amounts to 5,000, which gives a proportion of eighteen communicants for every hundred baptized persons. 5. Ten thousand children, of whom 7,000 are children of Chris tian parents, (nearly 4,000 of them boys, and upwards of 3,000 girls,) are receiving the benefits of a Christian education in our Mission schools.*

I should here explain that in all these statistics I have preferred to employ round numbers, as being most easily remembered ; but the exact numbers are somewhat over, not under, what I have stated.

6. Boarding Schools, Training Schools, and educational insti tutions of various kinds have also been set in operation for the training up of native schoolmasters and catechists, and eventually, it is hoped, for the raising up an indigenous ministry, and already, eleven Hindus, ten of whom are natives of the province, have been admitted by ordination to the ministry of the Church of England in Tinnevelly.

7. Progress has also been made towards self-support towards the support of the Christian institutions of the province by the zeal and liberality of the natives of the province themselves. Much, it is true, remains to be done in this direction before our native congregations stand alone without foreign aid, and possibly some things remain to be un-done; but, undoubtedly, real pro gress has been made, for if the funds which are now contributed by our native Christians to the various religious and charitable Societies that have been established amongst them, were all directed into the one channel of the sustentation of ordinary parochial institutions, they would amply suffice for the support of one native clergyman, and four native schoolmasters for

each of the twenty districts into which the province has been divided.

In these results we see unquestionable proofs of progress, and have been furnished with abundant reasons both for thankfulness to God and for determining to go forward with energy, in His name and strength, in the doing of what remains to be done.

It must not be supposed that all the results that have now been stated, have been accomplished by the Society for the Pro pagation of the Gospel alone ; about two-thirds of all these results must be placed to the credit of the Church Missionary Society, which, as I have already mentioned in my introductory lecture, labours harmoniously in conjunction with the Society for the Pro pagation of the Gospel. It should also be borne in mind, that whilst the light of the Gospel burns in Tinnevelly with especial brightness, none of the adjacent provinces has been left in total darkness.

It now remains that I should give a detailed description of our missionary work in Tinnevelly ; but before entering into details, it seems desirable to give a general view of some of its characteristic features, especially such as tend to account for the results that have been accomplished.

Much of the success realized in Tinnevelly has been owing to the personal influence of the Missionaries; and I am naturally led by what I have said respecting the introduction of the pa rochial system, to mention this here, for it is only by means of the parochial system that the personal influence of the Minister of Christ can systematically cooperate with the influence of the truth.

The Missionaries in Tinnevelly have not taken up their abode in large towns, and contented themselves with occasional or periodical tours in the country, as has generally been done in Northern and Western India, but have lived and laboured in the smaller villages, in the heart of the country, amongst the un sophisticated peasantry ; and a considerable proportion of their success appears to be owing to their having thus followed the leadings of Providence, sought out those who really had " ears to hear," and endeavoured to bring their teaching and influence to bear on those classes which experience has proved to be the most accessible. If the Hindus were usually or easily influenced by arguments addressed to the intellect, the large towns, abounding with an intelligent population, would afford the most promising openings for missionary labour ; but there are scarcely any people in the world so indifferent to truth in the abstract, so destitute of loyalty to conscience, so habituated to let their convictions and actions go in different directions, as the Hindus ; whilst there are scarcely any who yield more readily to the wish of superiors, the influence of friends, or the example of those whom they are accustomed to follow. This is, no doubt, a weak point in their character ; but it shows the importance of endeavouring to gain their confidence, and acquire influence over them, if we wish to do them good. Now, in large towns, the personal influence of the foreign

Missionary is as nothing compared with the force of public opinion and the influence of the heads of caste. Even in Europe, there is no solitariness so intense as that of the stranger in a large city ; it is still more intense in India, where every approach to intimacy is fenced round by caste restrictions. The strength of caste is in proportion to the density of the population, and the influence of European Missionaries is in inverse pro portion to the strength of caste. In the villages and hamlets in the interior of the country, among which the Missionaries in Tiunevelly have preferred to labour, it is astonishing how much personal influence they have generally acquired, and how much they have been able to effect by means of that influence, especially in the neighbourhood of the place in which they reside. All the people within a circuit of ten miles at least, know inti mately the European Missionary and his family. They learn his views, objects, and plans; they acquire confidence in his charac ter ; they become convinced, from his manner of life and his readiness to do them all the good in his power, that the religion he teaches must be a good religion. In time, they cease to think of him as a foreigner ; they begin to value and follow his advice ; they learn to regard him as " a teacher sent from God ;" and at length, impelled by a variety of considerations, amongst which confidence in his character is one of the strongest, they place themselves formally " under Christian instruction," and under his pastoral care. Thus the Missionary's personal influence, which in large towns is so insignificant, in the smaller villages, and amongst a simpler, more primitive people, is found to be an important element of success. Whilst the threefold cord resists every effort, the cords taken separately are easily broken. In connexion with all Societies that have stations in the cities and large towns, it has been found that the usual routine of preaching and distributing tracts to casual passers-by in crowded thoroughfares, and at still more crowded festivals, and superin tending small vernacular schools taught by native schoolmasters, has been attended with very insignificant results ; and apparently for this reason, that personal influence the influence of character, station, and neighbourhood on which so much depends amongst Hindus, is in this system scarcely brought into action at all. This view is confirmed by the circumstance that in those schools and colleges of a superior order established in some of the great towns, and in which the Missionaries themselves are the teachers, the influence they have acquired over the minds of their pupils has been attended with remarkable results. I have no doubt, therefore, that much of the success realized in Tinnevelly is owing to the fact that the Missionaries have availed themselves of the facilities for influencing the agricultural classes which have been found to exist, secluded themselves from European society, buried themselves in the palmyra jungles in search of Christ's lost sheep, and made homes for themselves, not where ideas of comfort and refinement would dictate, but where their work lay, and where they have found their reward. In connexion with this topic, I should mention another im portant purpose which our parochial organization helps us to accomplish. Kegarding ourselves as pastors of the entire com munity residing within our districts, and remembering that we are commissioned to " preach the Gospel to every creature," and to " make disciples of all nations," we are accustomed to invite all within our districts to place themselves at once under our pastoral care, without distinguishing between the promising and the unpromising, or waiting till the unpromising show signs of improvement, and to form such persons at once into Christian congregations, subject to the discipline and training suitable to catechumens. We believe that the adoption of this system is involved in obedience to our Lord's command, " Preach the Gospel to every creature " " disciple, baptize all nations" We believe that if we are to disciple "all," we have no right to receive the promising, and reject the unpromising, at our own discretion that we have no right to leave to their fate any who are willing to learn the Truth, however backward they are likely to be in learning it ; and that if we would teach all, the best way the only scriptural way to proceed is, to " disciple " them, according to Christ's own injunction, that is, to form them into congregations of "disciples," under systematic instruction and pastoral care, baptizing them on their profession of faith, and " teaching them to observe all things whatsoever Christ has commanded." Of those who in this way assume the Christian name, many doubtless will cause us disappointment by their evil tempers and conduct, through whom the way of truth will be evil spoken of; but we must not, and do not, through fear of this or any other difficulties, presume to cast out any who are willing to receive instruction. In no other way than by hearing, learning, and believing the Divine Word can sinners be con verted ; in no other way can the mass be purified than by commixture with the leaven ; and the " leaven " referred to in our Lord's parable is not truth in the abstract, but " the king dom of heaven," truth embodied in the Gospel Church ; which leaven was not to be kept separate from the meal, as some now- a-days would wish it to be, but " hid in it, till the whole should be leavened." In some quarters heathens are exhorted, simply and abstractly, to repent of their sins and believe the Gospel, without being urged to join themselves at once to the Church of Christ. The Missionary will allow them to attend his congregation, as hearers ; but he does not urge them to attend, and he is reluctant to receive them under his pastoral care, even as catechumens, until their motives are thoroughly scrutinized, and he is assured that the elements of the Christian character are already developed. He is afraid of compromising the credit of his cause by "receiving sinners." It is as if a surgeon, placed in charge of a hospital, should make a selection amongst the sick, and restrict himself to the treatment of favourable cases, declining to receive under his care any whose recovery was unlikely, and should defend his adoption of the system by pleading the necessity of maintaining the credit of the institution. Wheresoever this eclectic system has been acted upon, the results have proved unsatisfactory. It cannot be expected that Christ will bless a system which pretends to be wiser and more spiritual than His own, and which, instead of discipling " all nations," aims only at discipling a select num ber of the well-disposed and promising of all nations. The Mis sionaries in Tinnevelly have not been deterred by any fear of consequences, or regard for popular prejudices, from acting up to the letter of their Lord's command, "discipling" all who are willing to place themselves under their care, instructing every one who will consent to receive instruction, forming catechumena everywhere into congregations, and teaching them that " he that believe th and is baptized shall be saved ;" and to this mode of working the success that has been realized is doubtless, in part at least, to be attributed. In whatever way other classes may be Christianized, no system but this is adapted to the conversion of the illiterate, the un thinking, the lower classes generally, the very young and the very old, all of whom, prior to their reception within the pale of Christian influences, are equally unpromising and incapable of acting for themselves. When such persons know not only what they are to think and believe, but what they are to prac tise when it is not left to their own judgment what course they should adopt, on feeling convinced of the truth of what they are told when they are informed that if they would learn the way of salvation, and walk in it, they must attach themselves to the Christian congregation of the neighbourhood, and submit themselves to the guidance and care of the Missionary of their district, whom they are to regard as one who has been appointed to watch for their souls they are relieved from perplexity, and the obligation of embracing Christianity is felt with greater practical force.

The perception of this obligation is found to be strengthened by the practice, universal in Tinnevelly, of assembling the Christian inhabitants of every village, every morning and even ing, for public prayer and catechization. There are one or two full services weekly, besides the Sunday services, in every station where a Missionary resides, when the entire service for the day is read, and a sermon preached ; but at the ordinary morning and evening prayers to which I now refer, and which are con ducted by the native teachers in the various villages of a district, we are content with an abbreviation of the prayers, such as would be read at family worship, together with the psalms, or one of the lessons, and a brief catechization t or exposition. Catechiza tion, or catechetical instruction of some kind, is never omitted, morning or evening, and forms everywhere the chief means in use for training up our people in divine knowledge. Generally, the native teacher teaches the people only one subject a week, a subject appointed by the Missionary in accordance with some general plan of instruction, and the people are examined as to their acquaintance with it on the occasion of the Missionary's next visit. This reiteration of the same lesson is found to be necessary if we wish the mass of the people to make real pro gress ; for the same persons are not present every day, and even if they were, we find we must repeat the same statement fre quently, " line upon line, and precept upon precept," and put it before their minds in different lights, before the majority of them thoroughly comprehend it. In general, the women alone attend prayers in the morning, when the men are out at work in their fields, and the men alone in the evening, after the work of the day is over, when the women are engaged in preparing the evening meal, the principal meal of the day. All children, however, attend both morning and evening, and there are a few older people here and there, who, like " Anna the prophetess," " depart not from the temple day or night."

One important advantage arising from this system is that, though the great majority of our Tinnevelly Christians are naturally dull of comprehension, they are steadily and manifestly growing in divine knowledge, and in many cases will more than bear a comparison with persons of a similar position in life in our English congregations. Another advantage is, that the Christian inhabitants of the same village, assembling together morning and evening in the same place, and being catechized together, learn to consider themselves, though perhaps of different castes, as one community, one family in the Lord. A circumstance of not less importance is, that in this way the existence and vitality of the little Christian congregation is made known to every person in the neighbourhood ; it is enabled to " hold forth the word of life," to testify its belief in unseen things, to bear its part in "condemning the world of the ungodly:" and not only does it condemn the ungodly, but it attracts the reflecting ; for the very fact of the native converts assembling together every morning and evening to worship God, is an invitation to every one who has " ears to hear," and the voice of praise and prayer ascending daily from the humble village church, says "COME!" to all the neighbourhood. The surrounding heathen too often refuse to be made acquainted with the doctrines of Christianity ; but they cannot refuse to become acquainted with the visible embodiment of those doctrines in the Christian Church. The Church's unity, her discipline, her zeal for justice and truth, her care for her poor members, her exertions in behalf of the oppressed, her unwearied instructions, her daily prayers, her solemn services, her corporate life, her progressive prosperity, her universal claims these cha racteristics of the Church render her visible in Tinnevelly, even to heathen eyes, " a city set upon a hill, which cannot be hid ;" and it is unquestionable that these signs of life attract and influ ence the Hindu mind more than abstract truth is found to do.

In sketching the characteristics of the Tinnevelly Missions, an important place should certainly be assigned to the system of daily prayer and instruction to which I have referred, and also to the moral training and religious oversight and discipline which have grown up together with it, and which would be impracti cable without it. I am persuaded that nowhere in the world whether in Missions to the heathen, or in countries long ago Christianized, and in connexion with no church or religious organization in the world is there to be found in actual opera tion at the present time a system of instruction and oversight more complete and comprehensive than that which is at work in our Tinnevelly Missions. In those Missions, at least in every village which has been under Christian training for an adequate space of time, every individual, young and old, has his weekly lesson in divine knowledge to learn, and is periodically examined as to his progress in it ; nearly every child of Christian parents, male and female, is in school ; and every offence against morals and religion, whether committed by a baptized person or by a catechumen, is formally inquired into, either by the Mis sionary or by the heads of the village, and visited by the penalties of the local Christian law. That system of " godly discipline," the want of which the Church annually laments in England, is in full operation in Tinnevelly, and its watchful eye is ever on the convert, at home as well as in church, and at his work as well as [in his disputes and amusements. Dr. Duff, who visited Tinnevelly in 1849, particularly noticed the com pleteness, fatherly strictness, and " earnest workingness " of the system of instruction and discipline he found there, and com mented upon it in terms of admiration at the Anniversary meeting of the Church Missionary Society. It would not be right, how ever, to ascribe the benefits of this system solely to the Mission aries by whom it has been introduced, though I think they have shown that they had a clear perception of their duty as the founders of a new Christian community ; still greater credit is due to the people under our care, with whose consent and con currence this system was introduced, by whose aid, in a very great degree, it has been carried into effect, and who have proved, in the majority of cases, by their obedience to the rules of the Christian municipality, and their reverence for the authority of their pastors, that they really are a docile and tractable people, who, whatever be their present condition, may be expected to rise to a better one, and to occupy an eminent position hereafter among Hindu Christians.

The effects of this system of religious instruction and moral training and discipline are highly beneficial in a variety of ways. The surrounding heathens, perceiving the order, intelligence, and unity of the native Christian Church, and knowing that she professes to be fighting against idolatry, under the banner of a Divine Leader, cannot but feel secretly convinced that she is destined to win the day. Being themselves split into innu merable castes and sects, and agitated by intestine feuds, without order or discipline, without any common bond of authority, or code of faith, held together only by mechanical agglutination, or the fossilizing cement of age and indolence, the Hindus cannot but feel arrested and attracted by signs of life and growth, of discipline and energy, such as they look for in vain among their own worn-out creeds. The trained intelligence, and organized coherence and strength of the Christian community, cannot but produce in their minds, at least in the minds of the observant and reflecting, a favourable impression. If they gave utterance to their impression in words, they would exclaim, with Balaam, when from the mountain tops he beheld in the plains beneath him the orderly encampment of the Israelites, " How goodly are thy tents, Jacob, and thy tabernacles, Israel ! The Lord his God is with him, and the shout of a king is among them !" To give a distinct idea of the constitution and management of the Missions in Tinnevelly, it is necessary here to give some ex planation both of the Indian village system, and of our Catechist system, each of which has furnished peculiar facilities both for systematic instruction and for the exercise of discipline.

The village system of India is one of the most remarkable features of Indian civilization. Generally, the civilization of the Hindus is inferior to our own, but in some particulars it is in advance of ours ; and one of the particulars in which it claims the advantage is the fact that every Hindu village is an organized municipality. The greater number of English towns, and all English villages, are mere collections of houses, without any bond of connexion or corporate life, without rulers, without office bearers, and without any organization for the preservation or advancement of the common interests. In India, on the con trary, every village of any respectability is an incorporation. It has its council of head men, its rights of jurisdiction, its revenues, and its meetings for the transaction of public business. Gene rally, every village has its watchman, its artificers, its priests, its astrologer, appointed by the community, and paid by means of endowments or rates ; it has also a village moonsi/ (or petty unpaid magistrate), a mirdsddr or potail (a sort of mayor and revenue commissioner), and an accountant, all nominated by the community, and appointed by Government. The municipality ordinarily makes itself responsible for the settlement of disputed claims by arbitration, for the punishment of petty offences, and for the preservation of the peace ; and though courts and cut- cherries have been established in every province for the administration of justice on the European plan, nine-tenths of all the cases that arise are investigated and settled by the heads of the village under the council-tree, without any reference to Govern ment authorities ; and it is astonishing how much legal skill, how much judgment and good temper, these village punckdyets exhibit. The decisions of the heads of the village carry no legal force ; they cannot be carried into effect without the consent of the parties concerned and this is an important safeguard against abuse ; but they are almost invariably accepted and submitted to when they are believed to be just and are supported by the public opinion of the neighbourhood ; and in most instances the only appeal that is made is from the decision of one village to that of another and more distant village.

This municipal organization is so ancient and firmly established, that it may be regarded as the most permanent institution in India. Dynasties have arisen and fallen, religious sects and schools of philosophy have flourished and disappeared, but the village muni cipality retains its place undisturbed. One race of conquerors after another has swept over the country ; but as soon as the wave has passed, the municipality emerges again to view: every man returns to claim his rights, and the old landmarks are restored. In the Hindu's eyes, the nation occupies but a small place, the dynasty a still smaller one ; the institutions which he regards as all-important are his caste and his village, and it is in these that all his feelings of patriotism centre. That love of home, that attachment to the same spot, that disinclination to emigrate, that certainty we feel respecting every Hindu who has left home, that, sooner or later, he will return and spend his earnings in his native place, are to be attributed, in great part, if not altogether, to the influence of the village system of India.

The same system has contributed largely to the consolidation, if not to the extension, of Christianity in our rural Missions generally, but especially in Tinnevelly, where we have systema tically availed ourselves of its help. When a Tinnevelly village embraces Christianity, it immediately forms itself, almost as a matter of course, into a Christian municipality, and authorizes its head-men to exercise a genera_ superintendence over the con gregation, and, in conjunction with the native teacher or Catechist, to carry into effect the Missionary's views. Even in those cases where only a portion of a village becomes Christian, and that not the most influential portion, it forms itself, not only in ecclesias tical and educational matters, but even in the greater number of social matters, into a new municipality, and generally manages to maintain its independence. The heads of a congregation, being also the heads of the community, have much more power and a much wider scope of influence than English churchwardens, and where they happen to be really good, prudent men, are immea surably more useful to the Minister. They feel themselves re sponsible for the obedience of the rest of the people to Christian rules, for their regularity in attending church and sending their children to school, for the collection of contributions for charitable and religious purposes, for carrying into effect decisions of Church discipline, as well as for the settlement of any civil and social dis putes that may arise. The head-men may be said to hold their appointment by hereditary right, or in virtue of their position in society ; for though they are chosen by the people, and appointed by the Missionary, yet in almost every instance those persons alone are appointed to whom the people have always been accus tomed to look up ; and thus the head of the village is also the elder in the congregation.

So long as Christianity has not acquired a recognized footing in a village, but is only seeking an entrance, the corporate action of the community is undoubtedly a serious obstacle to its pro gress ; for the heads of villages sometimes abuse their power, and place might before right in their dealings with the poorer mem bers of the community, and when this is the case they naturally fear, that the influence of the European Missionary, and the intro duction of an authority independent of their own, will tend to check their oppressions and restrain their power within legal limits. It is from this source that those persecutions proceed which almost invariably take place on the first entrance of Chris tianity into a village.

When once, however, a village, or any considerable portion of a village, has embraced Christianity, and the Christian head men have won for themselves a tolerably firm position, it is astonishing in how large a degree this village system furthers the establishment of Christian laws and usages, and the con solidation of a Christian congregation into a regularly organized Christian community. When anything goes wrong in a con gregation, the Missionary appeals to the elders and head-men to restore things to rights j whereupon they assemble the people, or go from house to house, and endeavour to effect a re formation. There is rarely any danger of their setting the Missionary's authority aside, and using their power in opposition to him. Practically, the only danger that exists lies in the opposite direction. The Missionary's influence in his own dis trict being much greater than that of any other person, the people of every congregation, the head-men included, are prone to refer every case to him, instead of settling it amongst them selves: a tacit conspiracy is thus entered into to make him a universal "ruler and divider ; " and if he is young and inexpe rienced, he will probably fall into the temptation, until his patience is wearied out with disputes and litigations (a large crop of which is continually ripening in a country where illiterate peasants are the proprietors of the soil, and where all property is held in hereditary coparcenery) ; whereas if he steadily makes it his aim to develop the capacity for self-government which every congregation of any size is found to possess, and to organize some central court of appeal, such as the niydya sabei, or " council of justice," which we had in Edeyenkoody, and which was composed of five householders, annually chosen by the whole people, he is set free to devote his time and strength to the spiritual work of his office, with only a general directive influence in the adminis tration of temporal affairs, and the interests of the people them selves are in the end more effectually advanced.

I must now give some explanation of our Catechist system. This system is not peculiar to Tinnevelly, but has been introduced, more or less, in all Missions to the heathen, whether they be Roman Catholic or Protestant, Episcopal or non-Episcopal. The extent, however, of our Tinnevelly Mission brings out the Catechist system into greater prominence there than elsewhere, and gives it more of the character of an essential feature of our Missionary work. When an European Missionary establishes himself in a new sphere, he generally finds it necessary to engage a few educated Christian natives to assist him in making Christianity known in the surrounding country, to go before him when he purposes visiting a village in order to invite the people to come and listen, and to follow up his address by instructing more fully, and in greater detail, those who are willing to learn. When the Missionary begins to make an impression in the neighbourhood, and Christianity has effected an entrance into village after village, the assistance of native teachers becomes still more necessary than before; for in most parts of Tinnevelly, Christianity finds the entire mass of the people unable to read and without a school, and much work requires to be done which the Missionary cannot himself overtake, and that at one and the same time, in many different and distant villages. As soon as a few families in a village have agreed to abandon their idols, and to place themselves under instruction, it is necessary that they should be formed into a con gregation, and systematically instructed in everything that a Christian should know. Accordingly, a Catechist, or native teacher, is sent to reside amongst them, to teach them their daily lessons in Scripture history and Christian doctrine, to assemble them every morning and evening for prayer and catechization, to instruct them in the habits and usages suitable to a Christian community, to teach their children to read, and, in addition to all this to endeavour to win over to Christianity those who remain in heathenism in that and neighbouring villages. In most of the smaller congregations the same person is both Catechist and Schoolmaster ; but when the congregation increases, a division of labour becomes necessary, and then the Catechist's work assumes more of the character of the work of the Ministry. The native word which we render " Catechist" means simply an " instructor," and is altogether different from that by which the ordained Minister is denoted ; besides which, the Catechist con fines himself in his ministrations to those things which are com petent to a layman ; so that, although up to a certain point his work resembhles the Clergyman's, it is not liable to be confounded with it. When the Missionary visits any congregation, in his pro gress from village to village throughout his district, he himself reads the service, preaches, catechizes, examines the school, con verses with the people, holds interviews with the heathen ; all that is to be done, he does himself then and there, with the exception, perhaps, of the administration of the Sacraments, which are ordinarily restricted to the mother church in the central station ; but during the interval that must elapse before another visit is paid, how is the Missionary's place to be supplied ? The interval may last several weeks, in some places several months ; and during that period the native teacher com municates to the people all that he has been taught by the Missionary at the weekly meeting of Catechists, and diffuses around him the influences which he has received. Without the Catechist, (until such time, at least, as a duly-qualified native ministry shall be raised up,) no systematic instruction, no sys tematic guidance would be possible ; illiterate, low-caste converts would have to be abandoned in despair ; no progress could be made, even by the most promising congregations, towards self- government, self-support, or any other sign of maturity ; and even the raw material of a native ministry could never come into existence. It is our hope, indeed, that many of our native Catechists will in time be transformed into ordained native Ministers, supported by their own native flocks ; and in our various arrangements that object is kept steadily in view, and is, or ought to be, systematically worked for ; but as only a very small number of the native teachers have as yet been ordained, or evinced such qualifications and such a style of character as would justify their ordination, and as we have not yet the means of supporting a very large number, the employment of inferior men in a subordinate capacity cannot, as yet, be dispensed with. Some time must yet elapse before the Seminaries and Training Schools send out an adequate supply of men who are duly qualified even for the subordinate posts of Schoolmaster and Catechist, and some time must also elapse before the more promising persons employed in those subordinate offices are tested, strengthened, and ripened for the superior and more sacred functions of the Ministry ; but the time will, I have no doubt, come, and is coming, for already eleven Catechists have been ordained in Tinnevelly alone, and whilst we are waiting and working for the higher good, we thankfully avail ourselves of the lower; we use the lower, indeed, as a means of rising to the higher.

Our native Catechists are carefully trained for their work, not only before they are sent out, but during the whole period of their employment. Many of those who have hitherto been in employ ment had few or no educational advantages in early youth ; for it is only of late years that our Training Seminary was established. They could read and write when they were first employed, but that was all ; but every Missionary devotes an entire day every week to the instruction and training of his Catechists in their vernacular tongue, and some of them have now made considerable progress in every department of theological knowledge ; so that if their piety, zeal, and energy were equal to their intelligence, they might be ordained at once. In addition to instructing my Catechists in various branches of necessary knowledge, it was my custom to give them every week an outline of the sermon which I intended to preach on the fol lowing Sunday ; explaining to them at length, or calling upon them to explain, how each part of the outline should be filled up. Then, not only was this sermon preached on the Sunday to each of the twenty-four congregations comprised in my district, but it was also used, throughout the following week, as the basis of catechization at morning and evening prayers ; and whenever I visited a village, I was accustomed to question the people, to see how much they had retained of the various discourses that had been addressed to them. One year all the Missionaries, by mutual agreement, instructed their Catechists, and through them the people, in Bishop Pearson's masterly book on the Creed ; and I have heard many of our people say that they had never had so clear an idea before of the symmetry and grandeur of the Chris tian system. The Seminary for training up Catechists and Schoolmasters, which was founded in Sawyerpuram by the Rev. G. U. Pope, and which is now under the care of the Rev. H. C. Hux table, has begun to furnish us with a supply of youths who have been educated in English, and, through the medium of English, in the higher departments of learning ; and from amongst the new order of Catechists thus supplied to our Mis sions, we may fairly expect a body of well-educated, useful native Ministers to be raised up.

The employment of native teachers would not be practicable to such an extent as it is, were it not for the social and economic facilities which India affords. So great is the value of money in Tinnevelly, and so few openings are there for the skilled labour of educated young men belonging to the middle and lower classes, that the services of almost any number of persons, respectably connected and possessed of the rudiments of education, can be obtained for any purpose for which they are required, for the insignificant sum of from 51. to Wl. per annum. There is often a difficulty in obtaining for the office of Catechist a person of adequate piety, steadiness of character, and energy ; but the difficulty is a moral one, not also, as it would be in this country, a pecuniary one.

It may possibly be supposed by some persons that the employ ment of laymen in such duties as I have described is uneccle- siastical. It should be remembered, however, that we should be most happy to supersede native Catechists by native Ministers, if men of the proper qualifications could be supplied to us in suffi cient numbers, and if we could raise the large additional funds that would be required for their support ; for SQL per annum is the lowest stipend which has yet been paid to any native Min ister, and this averages five times as much as the salary of a Catechist, and five times as much as there is any prospect of the majority of our hamlet congregations being able to raise. It should, therefore, be remembered that, in the great majority of cases, the choice lies not between lay Catechists and an or dained Ministry, but between lay Catechists and no ministry at all. The people who have become Christians are poor, generally un able to read, residing in small scattered villages and hamlets, and exposed to much petty persecution from their heathen neighbours. They were brought up in idolatry or demonolatry, deeply imbued with heathen notions and habits, profoundly ignorant of the most rudimental facts in history and morals, and but recently converted to Christianity. Under these circumstances, an occa sional visit from an ordained Missionary, whether European or native, (and nothing beyond an occasional visit is practicable at present,) would not meet the necessities of the case. If they are ever to become Christians worthy of the name, they must be trained, guided, and systematically taught, and this can be done at present only by a resident Catechist. This being the case, so far from the employment of laymen being unecclesiastical, it would, I think, be unecclesiastical as well as unscriptural to hesitate for a moment to employ them ; for all ecclesiastical pre cedents from the brethren in Apostolic times who " went every where preaching the word," and the brotherhoods and sisterhoods of the mediaeval period, down to the Scripture-readers and paro chial schoolmasters of our own times prove this, that the Church's " feet have been set in a large room ;" and the only exceptions to this are such as prove the rule, by proving for our warning how much has been irretrievably lost to our own branch of the Church by morbid scrupulosity about the employment of laymen in subordinate offices and the adaptation of means to varying circumstances and times.

In many poor, populous country parishes in England, I have noticed the existence of hamlets situated at a considerable distance from the parish church ; and I have too often found on inquiry either that Christianity had no visible, corporate existence in those outlying hamlets at all, and that the people were destitute of accessible means of grace, or that the only Christianity they had was nourished by a little Methodist chapel. It was impossible to avoid contrasting this state of things with the arrangement which would have been made in similar circumstances in Tinnevelly. There the hamlet would be an affiliated out-station of the parish church. A layman, a man of the people, (perhaps a small farmer, or a small shopkeeper, trained and guided by the Minister of the parish, and perhaps partially supported by parochial funds), would be acting as the Clergyman's representative, collecting the people daily in the little oratory of the hamlet a separatist chapel no longer for prayer and praise and spiritual instruction, preaching to them every Sunday the Clergyman's sermon, and accompanying them on special occasions, as at Christmas and Easter, to the parish church. I need not stop to inquire whether some still better arrangement than this might not be discovered ; but surejy~, in comparing even this with the arrangement, or rather the no-arrangement, which one generally finds in England, it is not without reason that I maintain that our Tinnevelly plan is of the two decidedly to be preferred.

I have mentioned some circumstances which have contributed to the reception of Christianity by various classes of people in Tinnevelly, and some which have contributed to the consolidation and growth of the new Christian community. My sketch would be far from being perfect, and the impression I produce would be far from being accurate, if I said nothing respecting the motives which have induced many of the people to place themselves under our care. Wherever we have gone, we have preached to the people the Gospel of Christ, in accordance with Christ's own command; we have known nothing amongst them save Christ, and Him crucified, and it is unquestionable that the Gospel, without the help of any extraneous influences, has again and again proved itself " mighty through God to the pulling down of strongholds." Still, it is equally true, that in the greater number of instances the conversions that have taken place have been the result, not of spiritual motives alone, but of a combination of motives, partly spiritual and partly secular, the spiritual motives predominating in some instances over the secular, in others the secular predominating over the spiritual: and this holds true, not only with respect to Tinnevelly and the Missions of the Clrnrch of England, but with respect to every rural Mission in India, with whatever Society it may be connected, and whatever may be the idea of its condition which is commonly entertained. May I not add that this has held good of every conversion of tribes and peoples, as distinguished from the conversion of isolated individuals, which the history of the Church has recorded 1

When T admit (the word " admit " is scarcely a correct one, it would seem to show that we have ordinarily put the case in a dif ferent light, whereas we have never done so,) when I avow that secular motives have contributed to the results realized in Tinne- velly, I wish to preclude misapprehension in a very material point. I do not include in those motives the sordid desire of pecuniary gain. The motives to which I refer, though secular, are not sordid. Our Tinnevelly converts receive from us no pecuniary assistance whatever, and on their becoming Christians they are expected not to ask, but to give; and they do give, and that largely, to various religious and benevolent objects, and entirely support their own poor. In promoting the welfare of our converts we have never aimed at alluring heathens, by the prospect of temporal benefits, to connect themselves with our Missions, or to accept our teaching; and when individuals or villages have wished to bargain with us, as they have sometimes wished, that they will become Christians on such and such terms, we have invariably refused to have anything to do with such venal con versions. The desire of direct pecuniary benefits cannot, there fore, be the motive by which our people have been influenced.

The secular advantages obtained by our converts are such as naturally and necessarily flow from Christianity, or are of such a nature that the expectation of obtaining them would be quite consistent with the persuasion that Christianity is from God, and with the wish to be guided by its principles. The expectation of receiving from the Missionary of the district advice in per plexity, sympathy in adversity, and help in sickness, and of being at all times kindly inquired after and spoken to ; the desire of being connected with a rising, united body, which is guided by European intelligence, and governed by principles of Christian justice ; the expectation of being protected in some measure from the petty tyranny and caste pride of their wealthy neighbours ; the fact that the native Christians appear after a few years to acquire a higher standing in society, and to enjoy more peace and prosperity than fell to their lot when they were heathens; the desire of advancement on the part of the lower castes, who find that we consider them as capable of advancement, and teach them to feel that they are men, these feelings and desires, arising from the perception of the indirect benefits conferred by Chris tianity, have had more influence in the minds of the people than the expectation of receiving any direct worldly advantages ; and such feelings, though secular in their origin, are obviously quite consistent with sincere Christian faith.

Similar feelings are found to produce similar results in a greater or less degree in all Missions. For example, the offer of a superior English and scientific education, sufficient to qualify those who receive it for Government situations, is found to allure the sons of the more wealthy inhabitants of the great Indian cities within the sphere of Christian teaching and influence. The offer of medical advice brings another class within the reach of the Missionaries. In one particular, however, the manner in which the principle is acted upon in Tinnevelly appears less open to objection than in those cases. The secular advantages which are enjoyed by the converts in Tinnevelly are such only as naturally and neces sarily flow from the reception of Christianity, and are not held out beforehand to any class of persons as an inducement to them to submit to Christian teaching.

In giving our people, when oppressed, advice and assistance to the best of our ability, we have sometimes been blamed on the supposition that we have steppe,1 out of ^ur proper sphere. It has been held apparently that when the flock is oppressed, it is the duty of the shepherd to stand by silent and unconcerned, and to leave the result to chance or to the tender mercies of official wolves. I repudiate, however, this interpretation of our duty as Christian Pastors. With few and rare exceptions, in taking an interest in the oppressions to which our people were exposed, we have simply done that which it was our duty to do towards those to whom we stood in the relation of pastors and friends, that which no man of Christian feeling and benevolence could help doing. We could not help advising the perplexed, sympathising with the injured, encouraging the degraded to arise, "rejoicing with them that rejoiced, and weeping with them that wept." "We could not help saying with the apostle, " Who is weak, and I am not weak? who is offended, and I burn not?" Christianity has " the promise of the life that now is, as well as of that which is to come," and they whose office it is to introduce Christianity amongst a heathen people, and to lay the foundations of a Chris tian community, cannot properly be blamed for exhibiting the truth of each part of this promise, and proving that the religion they teach is man's best friend.

To return, however, to the motives by which persons have been induced to abandon heathenism. I repeat that it is undeniable that the temporal and social advantage of the Christian religion have made a deep impression on the minds of many ; and it is obvious that such advantages will appear to persons who are still in heathenism, and who have been accustomed to act on worldly principles alone in a more attractive light, and to carry greater weight, than any purely spiritual benefits. Accordingly, many persons have undoubtedly placed themselves under the pastoral care of the Missionaries, not so much through the desire of ob taining Christian instruction or salvation from sin, as through their desire for protection and sympathy, or through the influence of secular motives generally.

It is desirable to mention here, that what I have said respecting the influence of secular motives, refers exclusively to the reception of persons, in the first instance, under Chris tian instruction as catechumens, not to their subsequent re ception by baptism into the Christian Church. If a person wished to receive baptism, and it were certainly known that he was influenced by secular motives, I would never consent to desecrate the sign and seal of regeneration, by administering it to a person who was so obviously unfit to receive the spiritual blessing. In such cases our rule should be that which was ex pressed by Philip to the Ethiopian eunuch, " If thou believest with all thine heart, thou mayest." Even as respects the re ception of persons in the first instance under Christian instruction, it is a fact of great importance to the right understanding of this subject, that there are thousands upon thousands of heathens in Tinnevelly, whom all secular motives combined have failed to draw within the region of light. Consequently, where persons more or less influenced by such motives, have become Christians, it is not only possible but probable, that there has also been some secret operation of God's Holy Spirit in their minds, and some special arrangement of circumstances in His providential dealings with them, predisposing them to accept the offer of the Gospel. Rather we acknowledge with gratitude that this is in accordance with the good purpose of His goodness in every age.

There is another circumstance which it is equally important to remember. Whatever be the motives by which those who have placed themselves under instruction have been induced to listen and learn, whether because they had " seen the miracles," and approved of the teaching, or " because they had eaten," or ex pected to eat, "of the loaves," or, as often happens, through both sets of motives together, it is the Gospel of Christ's saving love, the message of reconciliation to God through the blood of Christ, and that only, which we have preached to them and taught them ; it is by the Gospel that we have reached their consciences, and gained their hearts ; and it is through the efficacy of the Gospel that they have been enlightened, washed from the impurities of idolatry, and raised to their present condition. Whatever in fluences may have brought any of them into connexion with us in the first instance, all the benefits they have derived from that connexion, and all that gratifies the mind, and awakens hope in our progress from station to station throughout the Province, are direct results of the preaching of Christ's Gospel, and the ad ministration of the ordinances and discipline of Christ's Church. We have not thought it necessary to prepare heathens for Christian teaching by any civilizing or educational system, or to make a distinction amongst them by any discriminative process. In the state in which we found them, in many respects a very unsatisfac tory state, and without preparation or p^lu^e, save that of learning their language, we have preached to them the words of life. "We have said, as we were commanded, " Thus saith the Lord, believe and ye shall live ;" and the results have proved the propriety of the course pursued. Of the persons who have embraced Christianity from mixed motives, partly religious, partly secular, such as those I have described, the majority are found to adhere to it after all excite ment from without has passed away, and learn to value Christ ianity for higher reasons. From time to time, also, we discover amongst them a few pure-minded, truth -loving persons, whom Providence had been preparing even in heathenism for the re ception of the truth, and for bringing forth the fruits of right eousness. The congregation, consisting perhaps of the inhabitants of an entire village, was brought in, as it were, by the tide, and yet after a time we discover amongst the sand and sea-weed not a few pearls of great price, fitted to shine hereafter in a kingly crown.

I now proceed to furnish some particulars respecting the interior economy of a Tinnevelly district. As there is little difference, even in details, and no essential difference, between one district and another, and as I am necessarily best acquainted with my own district, and most interested in it, it is the work of my own dis trict that I am about to describe ; but that will serve, I think, more or less to illustrate Tinnevelly missionary work in general. It was towards the end of the year 1841 that I arrived in Tin nevelly, and took up my abode at Edeyenkoody, which became from that time the nucleus of a new missionary district. Although the Missions of both the Church Societies, particularly those of the Society for the Propagation of the Gospel, were then in a much less flourishing condition than they are now, I was even then delighted with the signs of progress which I witnessed. I had already had nearly four years' missionary experience in connexion with the London Missionary Society, during which period I had been labouring in the city of Madras ; but, before my arrival in Tinnevelly, I had seen few signs of missionary progress. In Madras and the neighbourhood the native Christians connected with the various Missions were isolated individuals, not communi ties, and all taken together were not equal in number to the Christian inhabitants of a single Tinnevelly district. In the province of Tanjore, on my way to the South, I saw communities of native Christians, villages entirely inhabited by Christians ; but, at that time at least, they exhibited few appearances of reli gious vitality. In Tinnevelly, however, I not only found large communities of Christians, entire districts of country more or less Christianized, but I also found those communities characterized by ever-increasing energy, and by unequalled docility and liberality. I was so much delighted by what I then saw, though many things were still evidently unshapen and rudimental, that on preaching my first sermon in Tianevelly, in the Mission Church at Nazareth, I took for my text these words. (contained in the Epistle for the day,) " The night is far spent, the day is at hand." My impression that the day was about to dawn has not been fully realized it is not day yet the darkness is still sorely reluctant to give place to the light ; for, though 43,000 souls have " come to the light," and are learning, with more or less singleness of purpose, to " walk in the light," more than 1,200,000 souls, in that province alone, remain in wilful darkness still ; nevertheless, on comparing what now exists in Tinnevelly with what I found in it, I cannot but perceive reasons both for thankfulness for the progress already made, and for hoping that the dawn, though long deferred, will soon arrive. When I arrived in Tinnevelly there were but two districts in connexion with the Society for the Propagation of the Gospel, viz. Nazareth and Moodaloor, each of which was under the care of a Missionary ; but it had been determined that I should endeavour to form a third, which should comprise an outlying portion of the Moodaloor district, together with an extensive, more distant, and hitherto almost unknown tract of country. The field of labour on which I thus entered, lies along the southern shore of Tinnevelly, being about twenty miles in length, and, on an average, five miles in breadth, with a population of about 20,000 souls. It com mences about twenty miles from Cape Comorin, the hills above which are distinctly visible from my house. Christianity had been introduced, in the early period of Satyanadan's labours, into the eastern part of this district, or that part which is included in the great palmyra forest, and chiefly inhabited by Shanars ; but this neighbourhood was afterwards more wofully neglected than any other part of the old Tinnevelly Mission, and the great majority of those who had embraced Christianity, including, in many instances, entire villages, fell away from it, in the absence of pastoral care during the pestilence which ranged so violently all over the southern provinces about thirty years before my arrival.

After our Missions in Tinnevelly had been recommenced, and a Missionary had been located in Moodaloor, the few scattered con- gregations that remained were occasionally visited by a Missionary, and Christianity again began to extend towards the western part of the district. For several years before my arrival my district was periodically visited from Moodaloor, but no Missionary had statedly and continuously laboured in the district before my arrival, no Missionary had resided in it, and almost everything pertaining to parochial organization had to be built up in it from the foundation by myself. The district derives the name by which it is known amongst Christians from Edeyenkoody, the name of the village where I took up my abode, and where there is now the principal Christian congregation in the district. The meaning of the name " Edeyen koody," or properly, Ideiyan-kudi, is, " the shepherd's habitation." This was the name of the place before I went there, and before Christianity was known there ; it was not given to it, therefore, by me, as might have been supposed: still, I always thought it a very appropriate name for the residence of a Missionary-Pastor, and very suggestive of the duties which I was sent there to dis charge ; for I went there as " a shepherd," as a servant of that " good," that divine " Shepherd, who gave his life for the sheep ;"

and the purpose I had in view in going there was to endeavour to gather into Christ's fold the sheep for which He died. I wish I could add that the object I aimed at has been accomplished ; but whilst some have listened to the Good Shepherd's voice, the majority have preferred the dangers of the wilderness to the pasture and protection provided for them in the fold of Christ. There, as everywhere else, it has been found that " many are called, but few are chosen." Still there, as elsewhere, " God's Word has not returned unto Him void, but has accom plished that which He pleased, and prospered in the thing whereto He sent it." In the district committed to me I made it my business to become acquainted with every village and hamlet, arid, if possible, with every family, and endeavoured, by myself, and with the help of my native assistants, to make known to " every creature " the message of reconciliation to God through the blood of the Cross. There were two truths which I found by experience every one, however rude, could comprehend, and which every one, however hardened, could appreciate, and those truths I always took care to teach and enforce. The first was that the burden of guilt which every man feels that he carries about with him, and which false religions leave untouched, is removed by Christ, " the Lamb of God which taketh away the sin of the world," and by Him alone ; the second, that in the conflict with evil which every man must wage, if he would be saved, and in which false religions leave him to his own resources, the religion of Christ supplies him with the help he needs, inasmuch as it brings him into contact with God, and opens to him a channel of sanctifying grace in the supply of the Spirit of Jesus. In these truths is the substance of the Gospel, and I have found them everywhere, not only intelligible, but fitted to produce serious thought. Proofs of the folly of idolatry leave the heart and character unchanged, but virtue goes forth from these truths respecting Christ, to heal every one that believeth.

Whilst I endeavoured, in journeying from village to village, to preach the Gospel to every creature, it was also my endeavour to plant in every village the nucleus of a Christian congregation. As the Gospel is a revelation from God, so the Church is an institution of God, and neither should the Church be substituted for the Gospel, nor should it be supposed that the Gospel ignores the Church. Accordingly, wherever two or three agreed to accept the message of mercy, I formed them into a new congre gation, and commenced to "teach them all things whatsoever Christ had commanded."

Though it was not my privilege to gather into the Christian fold all for whose conversion I longed and laboured, I have reason to be thankful that I was not called, as some more earnest, more faithful labourers have been, in other parts of the field of the world, to labour in vain, and " spend my strength for nought, and in vain." On leaving my district for a season, about three years ago, on account of failing health, it was my privilege to make over to a younger Missionary, to tend and keep in my absence, a Christian flock of 2,672 souls persons who were not merely occasional hearers of the Gospel, but who had formally placed themselves under Christian instruction, and under my pastoral care, and whose names were in our church books as baptized persons or catechumens. On my arrival in the district thirteen years before, I found about 1,200 persons under my charge, some of whom had been transferred to iny care by the Church Missionary Society. The average number of accessions from heathenism during the period of my labours was, therefore* over a hundred a year. There were times in which there was no visible progress, and times of trial when new comers were sifted, and their numbers diminished ; but taking the entire period, and in the main, there was a visible ascent and progress, and during the last two years alone, the accessions amounted to 640. When we stand on the sea-shore, and look at the rising and falling waves, we may sometimes be in doubt for a time whether the tide is ebbing or flowing, but if we fix our eye upon a mark, and wait patiently for a while, our doubts will soon be removed ; just so, I may have felt doubtful for a particular year or half- year, whether the Christian cause was advancing or receding, but on looking back upon the whole period, and observing how the wave of Christian influences reached and passed over village after.village, I cannot now doubt that the tide was rising.

All the native Christians who were under my care when I left, did not reside in the same place, or form a single congregation: they were all inhabitants of the same district, but they resided in twenty-four different villages, scattered over a considerable extent of country j and though the greater number of them occasionally assembled in the mother-church in Edeyenkoody, on an average once in three months, as one fold under one shepherd, yet, properly speaking, they formed twenty-four different congrega tions, under the instruction of nearly as many native teachers. The largest congregation in the district is that of Edeyenkoody, where the mother-church is situated, where we have central, superior schools, where I resided, and from whence I visited the other villages in the district in succession. That congregation numbered upwards of 600, and I endeavoured to make it a model congregation, and the village itself, in all its arrangements, material as well as moral, a model village to the rest of the district. The next congregation, in point of numbers, was that of East Tavurey, which contained upwards of three hundred souls. The rest were small, some of them very small, congrega tions, averaging about eighty souls each, and differing one from another very widely in condition and prospects some of them centres of Christian light, and exercising an important influ ence in the neighbourhood, others unsatisfactory, and a source of anxiety.

Wherever there is a congregation, however small, our local Church Building Society, a society which depends for support entirely upon our native Christians, and receives no aid from Missionary Societies, or from Europeans, has erected in the village a little place of Christian worship, in some instances a church, more generally a church-school a little edifice, how ever plain and primitive, which may be used as a school during the day, and in which, not only on Sundays, but every morning and evening throughout the Aveek, old and young, men, women, and children may be assembled together to hear God's word, and to join in His worship. Most of those little edifices are very rude and mean, compared with the churches of Christian England, being generally built of sun-dried bricks, in the old Egyptian or Babylonian style, and thatched with palmyra leaves. I might almost be ashamed to call them " churches," were it not that each of these little edifices is, as its Tamil name, " Kovil," signifies, " God's house," inasmuch as they who assemble there meet in the name of God their Saviour, and as He has promised to be with them: I trust, therefore, it may be said of each of them, as of Zion, that " the Lord will recount, when he writeth up the people, that this man and that was born there." It is also deserving of mention, that the village church is invariably the best built, cleanest, airiest building in the village ; and if this rule continues to be adhered to hereafter if as civilization progresses, and the people learn to build better houses for themselves, church archi tecture continues to keep ahead of domestic architecture, the churches of Christian India may at length rival, as the heathen temples do already, the churches of Europe. Similar hopes may, I trust, be entertained respecting the progress of a more important species of ecclesiastical architecture the architecture of the spiritual church of India, the church of living stones.

In the village of Edeyenkoody itself, the building now used as a church, though spacious, and somewhat church-like, is only of a temporary order; but a permanent stone church, capable of accom modating 1,200 persons, is in progress; I am sorry to say, how ever, that for want of funds the progress it makes is far from being as rapid as I could wish. The plan of the church was kindly furnished me by the Secretary of an English Church Building Society ; and though the style is simple, yet, as it is to be a permanent, stone-built church, and a specimen of good church architecture to the rest of the district, as it is to accommodate 1,200 persons, and as building in stone is more expensive in that remote neighbourhood, than in some other places in India, the entire cost of the church will not be less, and may be more, than 800l. About 300. have already been expended, and the building has advanced only as far as the windows, so that I reckon that about 500l. more will be required.

I hope to obtain a certain proportion of this sum from time to time from our native Christians ; but although they are very liberal in proportion to their means, as will be shown in a subsequent lecture, yet, I have generally preferred directing all the contributions that they were able to give for church-building purposes into the channel of our local Church Building Society, a Society which has built and kept in repair about thirty small churches and schools in various parts of the district. I trust therefore, that some Christian friends in this country will have the kindness to help me to finish, in an appropriate style, a church which is so much required, and which is to be the mother-church and the model of a large circle of Mission churches. I should add, that it is a fixed rule of the Society for the Propagation of the Gospel not to make any grants for church building.*

Some persons will, doubtless, wonder how one Missionary could tend and guide twenty-four different congregations. The task is certainly a difficult one, and would have been quite impossible, but for the help of our native Catechists. Any one who knows what is involved in the care of a single congregation, however small, in this old Christian country, where all preliminary difficulties were overcome centuries ago, may form some conjecture, though still but a very inadequate one, of the work and care, the pressure of anxiety, the ceaseless succession of hopes and fears, of successes and disappointments, connected with so large a number of newly formed congregations, each consisting of converts from idolatry or demonolatry, or of the children of converts, and each surrounded by a darkness which comprehends it not, but is desirous of extinguishing it. For the first five or six years I had few native teachers of any kind to assist me, and such as The best way to send me contributions for this purpose will be to remit them through the Society, i.e. to send the donation to any of the Secretaries or Treasurers of the Society, with the request that it may be sent out to me.

I liad were persons who had had no educational advantages in their youth. By and by, however, I obtained the help of youths whom I selected from the most promising pupils in the village schools, or who had already entered upon the employments of life, and those I instructed and trained, in a sort of local training- school, as well as my other engagements would admit. A Training-School was subsequently established at Sawyerpuram for the training up of schoolmasters and Catechists for the benefit of all our districts in common ; and before I left Tinnevelly it had begun to supply us with native helpers of a superior class. During the whole of my residence in Tinnevelly, as mentioned already, I was accustomed to devote an entire day every week to the instruction and improvement of my Catechists, on which occasions I communicated to them all I wanted them to com municate to the people. I was thus enabled to multiply myself, as it were, and to discharge many of the duties of the pastoral office in some twenty-four different places at once.'

The catechetical mode of preaching which is adopted in Tinne velly is particularly well fitted to the present condition of things in our congregations. Let my reader accompany me for a moment to Edeyenkoody, and see for himself what our plan is, and how it works. It is Sunday morning, shortly after sunrise ; the peal of four gongs has rung out, and the people are assembled in church ; we enter and look around. No white face is visible save those of the Missionary and his family, no English word falls upon the ear ; but the order of the service is the same as our own, and the few points of difference that are apparent are such as explain themselves. The people are seated, not in pews or on benches, but cross-legged on the floor, some on mats, some without. The men sit on one side of the church, the women on the other ; the "readers," or educated portion of each sex, in front, the un educated behind j and there are two transepts, fully commanded by the preacher's eye, in one of which are seated the boys, in the other the girls. The chief peculiarities we notice in the course of the service are, that the responses are made by the whole mass of the people, perhaps in rather too loud a tone for English ears, and that during prayer the whole congregation, with the excep tion of a few old people and women with children, kneel on the hard floor, without hassocks and without support. I read out my text, and before I proceed farther, make sure that every one has heard it, by asking a few of the children, and of the people who cannot read, to repeat it to me aloud. When I divide the dis course into heads, or mention any particulars which I wish to impress upon the attention, or endeavour to clear up a difficulty, or enforce a truth by some familiar local illustration, I ascertain for myself, by questioning each class of people in succession, whether they understand, and are likely to carry home, the lessons they have been taught. Sometimes I question a particular indi vidual by name, more commonly a class ; and if the question I asked is not answered by those to whom it is put, I put it to class after class till it is answered, beginning, perhaps, with the school children, then asking the uneducated adults, and finally ques tioning the educated young people. Sometimes, if an erroneous answer is given, it leads to a clearer view of the truth itself, for, in that case, I not only tell the people that the answer is wrong, but point out to them in what respect it is wrong, and this is sometimes the most instructive part of the discourse.

In addition to all this catechizing, and whilst it is going on, you may hear a peculiar scratching sound arising from various parts of the church ; this proceeds from persons who are writing out notes of the sermon with the iron style on slips of palmyra leaf. I never knew any male member of our congregations remain silent when asked a question, if he were able to answer it; and sometimes, if the question is a very easy one, the answer will proceed from twenty different persons at once. The women, as is natural, are not so ready to reply as the men ; yet I do not think it advisable to let them escape altogether, but ask them a question now and then to keep their attention alive ; and in the smaller congregations, especially at the ordinary morning prayers, where there are few men present, they answer as freely as I could wish. This system would probably be found impracticable in this country. Many English people feel an unconquerable repugnance to allow their voices to be heard in public ; and even when they understand a thing, they get so confused and abashed, when ques tioned about it in a promiscuous assembly, that they would be unable, even if they were willing, to reply. The structure of the Hindu mind is very different. The Hindus are much less ex citable, and less apt to get nervous than we are ; so that if a Hindu only understands a thing, he is not liable to be put out by being asked to explain it. I fear few English congregations will ever bear to be publicly catechized ; and yet, on looking round upon an English congregation, I have often seen and felt deficiencies which nothing but catechization could supply, and have longed to ascertain, in our Indian method, before passing on to a new subject, whether what was said previously was understood.

Another excellent arrangement for the instruction of our people consists in our adult Sunday-schools. The majority of our Tinnevelly Christians were converted, not merely from idolatry, but from the gloomiest demonolatry ; they belonged, with few exceptions, to a poor, rude, and illiterate class of society ; and few of them were able even to read before their conversion. In con sequence of all this, their mental condition was dark and uncul tivated, and they stood in peculiar need of systematic instruction, not only in the principles, but in the details of Christianity and morality. This instruction is supplied by the adult Sunday- schools, which I have established wherever I could. The children are not forgotten on Sundays ; but as they are carefully instructed every day in the week, our chief attention on Sundays is claimed by, and given to, the adults.

In Edeyenkoody our Sunday morning service is held shortly after sunrise ; the afternoon service closes a little before sunset ; and the middle of the

day, which is too hot and uncomfortable for Divine service, being left
unoccupied, it is appropriated to the adult Sunday-school. It is noon, and
the gong has rung for school ; we re-enter the large temporary church,
where the school is held, and again look around. We find as large an
attendance, both of men and women, as at Divine Service in the morning ;
say from 100 to 120 adults, out of a population of 600 souls. They are all
seated, as before, on the floor of the Church, not in rows, however, as at
Service, but in ten or twelve separate semi circles, each of which forms a
class. The " readers " formed only one class at first, but they have now
increased to four, viz. two of men ; and two of women ; and the members
of these classes read, and are questioned upon, some book of Scripture,
chapter by chapter, besides repeating some portion from memory. Those
who are unable to read once the great majority, now a minority are arranged
into classes according to the amount of their knowledge, and are taught
portions of the Catechism, or Scrip ture texts arranged in a series, or a
summary of important facts and doctrines. In this country, Sunday-school
pupils are almost invariably children, and their teachers almost invariably
grown persons. In Edeyenkoody we see exactly the reverse ; the pupils are
the adult inhabitants of the village, farmers, traders, and labourers, including
the " head-men " themselves, and the teachers are their children or grand-
children, in some instances boys and girls who have not yet left school.
After setting all the classes to work, my wife and I go from class to class,
guiding the teachers or examining the pupils, as circumstances may require,
or sit down with one of the classes of readers, explaining to them the word
of God more perfectly. It is wonderful to see how patiently and good-
humouredly the older people submit to be taught by their juvenile teachers.
Though they look to the teacher for the words of the lesson, and repeat
them patiently again and again, until they know them by heart, it sometimes
happens that they have a clearer insight than their teacher into the meaning
of the lesson. The teacher depends, perhaps exclusively, upon his lesson-
notes, whilst per haps the pupil has had the meaning written in his heart by
the Great Teacher himself. We endeavour to teach words as well as things ;
for there are many " forms of sound words," in Scripture and out of it,
which every person ought to know ; nevertheless, it often happens that the
older people find it difficult to retain words in their memory, whilst they
have succeeded in grasping the idea, in which the substance of truth resides.
I was once examining a very old man, who wished to be baptized, and,
according to custom, I asked him, amongst other things, if he could repeat
the Belief, which I knew he had been taught. He made the attempt, but
after a few incoherent sentences, gave it up in despair. At length he raised
his hand, and said, " I'll tell you, sir, the meaning of it. We are all sinners,
and the Lord Christ undertook for us all, and if we believe in Him we shall
be saved ; I know that, and that is all I know." In this instance the poor

man had really learned much in learning a little; for the substance of saving truth, the kernel of the Gospel, was contained in his reply. Such of the members of the congregation as are able to read are expected to attend also a Bible class, which is held on a week-day. On Wednesday at noon, about the time when all work ceases in Hindu villages, on account of the extreme heat, and when every one seeks the shade for a couple of hours, we are accustomed to assemble the people in church for the Litany and a short sermon, when the attendance averages about half that of the Sunday. After the service is over, the readers remain for about half-an-hour, and then I give them a general idea of the meaning and connexion of the chapter which they are to prepare for next Sunday's class ; so that if I am to be out " in the villages " on Sunday, my absence may not be seri ously felt.

We have another service, with a sermon, every Friday ; but as Friday is the market-day in the neighbourhood, the village is nearly deserted the greater part of the day, and a noon-tide ser vice is impracticable. The service is therefore held in the evening, between sunset and the native hour of dinner ; and, on this occasion, though I invariably preside during the service, and take some part in it myself, the prayers are read, and a sermon is delivered, by one of the native Catechists. Friday, as I have mentioned already, is the day I spend with the Catechists, and the sermon to be preached on Friday evening by each Catechist in succession, on a subject given him by myself, is a part, and not, I think, the least important part of the course of training by which our native teachers are fitted for their duties. There are, of course, great differences in the character of the sermons that are then delivered some flimsy and weak, some high-flown, some solid and instructive ; but in this, as in everything else, I have noticed a great improvement ; and I have rarely heard better sermons anywhere than those which were delivered in his turn by Gnana-moottoo, a Catechist of mine who has just been ordained. It may be regarded as a matter of surprise, and looking at things from this distance, I feel surprised myself, that people who are not in any way dependent on the Missionary should submit, as our people out there do, to all the teaching and training, the church-going and school-going that I have here described ; and yet it is a fact, that they not only submit to it, but generally enter into the spirit of it, and co-operate in carrying it on with more or less heartiness and zeal.

The feeling of the community is so strongly in its favour, when it has not been prematurely forced upon them, when it is ad ministered in a kindly, considerate spirit, and when their honour as a community or as a caste has not been infringed, that even the most indolent and irregular members of the congregation feel themselves obliged to yield to rules. One of our rules is, that if any person remains away from church or from Sunday- school so long as to attract attention, it is my duty to send for him, that I may have the opportunity of giving him the reproof or warning that he needs. In this country I might send for an absentee, but would he come when he was sent for'? possibly he would regard my sending for him as a sufficient reason for never coming to church again. In Tinnevelly, however, when we send for a man, he comes ; and as some cases of negligence or irre gularity will always occur in a large village, I had a particular hour every week appropriated to this department of discipline, and on that occasion it was the duty of the " head men" of the village to be present, that their influence and authority might strengthen mine. Occasionally, but very rarely, some person who was more obstinate than usual, would refuse to come when he was sent for, but this was considered by all his neighbours as so highly improper a procedure, that he generally yielded before long to the current of public opinion, without rendering it necessary for the village authorities to "sit upon him" under the council-tree.

Wherever this system of catechetical instruction and congre gational discipline has been acted upon for any length of time, the best effects have been apparent. I feel confident that most of our Shanar and Pariar Christians in Tinnevelly, notwith standing their natural dulness, will be found to have a better knowledge of God's word, and of divine things generally, than the majority of persons belonging to classes and conditions con siderably superior to theirs, in connexion with English congre gations. As respects knowledge and order, docility, and liberality, " the preparation of the heart, and the answer of the tongue," they undoubtedly occupy a high position amongst Christians.

I am far, however, from undervaluing the indirect results of the transmitted Christianity of Europe results, of which the value is apparent, even in the rural districts, and amongst the labouring classes of this country j for when divine grace takes possession of an English peasant or of an English artizan, and his heart is touched by the constraining love of Christ, he rises at once, and almost without an effort, to a higher, more manly, more con scientious, more emotional, more enlightened style of piety than even Hindu converts of a superior order generally reach.

Whilst we have devoted much attention and effort to the instruction of the adult members of our Tinnevelly congre gations, we have not been forgetful of the still greater importance of the Christian education of the young. The rising generation is everywhere the hope of the Church, but especially so in a heathen country, in a recently-formed Christian community. I do not regard any portion of God's creatures as hopelessly degraded, but in a country where every moral principle has been contaminated and warped by a hundred generations of heathenism, where the very atmosphere seems to be tainted with impurity and deceit, there is certainly more hope of the young, whose minds are still tender and impressible, than of those who have grown old in sin, and who have been converted from the evil of their ways late in life.

With this conviction in their minds, the Missionaries have laboured hard for the benefit of the rising generation, and undoubtedly Christian education has made much progress in Tinnevelly progress very much greater than might have been expected amongst a class of people who had been content, in most instances, from the beginning of their history, to live in the grossest ignorance, and who, when we first became acquainted with them, neither desired nor appreciated any sort of education. Though, however, they were scarcely in a condition to appreciate the advantages of education, they were willing to believe that the Missionaries knew better than they what was good for themselves and their children ; they were willing to be guided and ruled j and the result has been, not only that the children of Christian parents have grown up an educated generation, but that edu cation is now generally appreciated by the parents themselves.

In many of the more important Christian villages in Tinnevelly, the proportion of the population in school amounts to one in four, or twenty-five per cent., a proportion which has not been, and indeed cannot be, exceeded in any country in the world. This proportion has not, indeed, generally been reached, and the educational condition of our smaller, poorer, outlying villages, is necessarily inferior to that of villages that are more populous and more prosperous ; yet the general average, in all our dis tricts taken together, reaches sixteen per cent., and the number of children, male and female, Christian and heathen, in the school-lists in the various Christian schools in the province, amounts to 10,000. In my own village, Edeyenkoody, the proportion of the population ;in school was fully one in four; and even when I took all the villages in the district, promising and unpromising, into the average, the proportion fell very little short of that. When I left the district, the number of native Christians of all ages under my care was 2,672: at the same period the number of children of Christian parents in the various schools that had been established throughout the district was

(300 boys and 275 girls) ; and in addition to this band of Christian children, 295 children of heathen parents were receiving as many of the advantages of a Christian education as they were willing to receive.

It is evident that in the education of a goodly band of children, a most important door of usefulness has been opened to the Missionary. Whatever opinion may be entertained of the older converts, and how unpromising soever the condition of some of them may be supposed to be, we have their children, at all events, in school, to bring up from the first in " the nurture and admonition of the Lord ;" and as the parents are uniler Christian instruction and pastoral oversight no less than the children, we have reason for hoping that the lessons of truth which are taught in the schoolroom during the day, will not be obliterated at night, when the children return home, as too often happens when the parents are heathen.

All the schools established in the district of Edeyenkoody, with the exception of a superior girls' school, of which I shall mention some particulars presently, are vernacular day-schools. There is much demand for an English education in the great towns of India, and since the Government grant-in-aid system was introduced, the demand has begun to spread even in the rural districts ; but, up to the time I left, a solid education in the vernacular language was all that seemed to be required by the people of my own district, and all that I endeavoured to provide for. I do not expect, indeed, that English will ever be much studied by that class of children that chiefly attended my schools. It is difficult in every country to induce the children of small farmers and farm-labourers to remain in school long enough to learn even their own tongue thoroughly ; and as English is in Tinnevelly a foreign tongue, and the study of it rather a scholarly accomplishment than a necessity, it will always be found, not only difficult, but impossible for the great majority of Shanar children to learn English. It is a consolation, however, that they are provided with a good supply of intellectual food in their own language. We had the Bible in Tamil three translations of the greater portion of it the Prayer-book, a printing press in every province, and an increasing and improving Christian literature. Our people are able to read in their own tongue God's " wonderful works," and His wonderful mercy ; and we find no difficulty in getting access, by means of that tongue, to their minds and hearts.

The education we give in our village schools, though in the vernacular language, is tolerably substantial: it comprises read ing, writing, mental arithmetic, catechisms of Scripture history and doctrine, a little geography, and a little High-Tamil poetry ; and if the children could only remain long enough in school to receive all the advantages which we are prepared to give them, we should not have much room left for regret.

Many things connected with the interior economy of our schools are of so primitive a character, that a stranger might be led to bestow upon us more pity than we require. When you enter any of our schools, you see most of the children very scantily clothed many of the little boys, indeed, with the smallest apology for clothing that an ingenious economy can invent. You find them also seated, not on forms, but cross-legged on the floor, learning to write, not with pen, ink, and paper, but first on fine sand spread out before them on the ground, and afterwards with the iron pen or graver on the palmyra leaf. The first books they use also are oleis, or written leaves of the palmyra ; and their arithmetical exercises are worked out, not on slates, but either on the olei, or in their heads. Notwithstanding these peculiarities, the children have the means of acquiring as solid and useful an education as the majority of children be longing to the same class of society in more highly favoured countries. I have always endeavoured, not merely to teach the mechanical art of reading, but to teach the children to think, to supply them with right principles of action, and teach them to act from right motives to pour the light of truth into their minds to win them to Christ to train them up for usefulness on earth, and for happiness in heaven ; and though, doubtless, it has sometimes happened that I have not been duly seconded in such endeavours by the native schoolmasters, and that even when all favouring circumstances concurred to inspire me with hope, the result has been sorrow, not joy, and I have appeared to have been labouring in vain ; yet, on the other hand, the good seed has not, in every instance, fallen upon a bad soil. Some who have been taught the way they should go, have not departed from it when they grew up ; the second generation of native Christians is, on the whole, superior to the first ; and the whole of our school children the promising and the unpromising alike have derived this advantage, at least, from the education they have received, that they have become more intelligent hearers of the Word of God, and more capable of receiving religious impressions, than they would otherwise have been.

I was accustomed to devote four days in succession every month to the examination of the schools. The children be longing to a particular class in each school were all assembled at once in Edeyenkoody ; a day was devoted to the examination of each class ; and as a portion of every school in the district was present, and the comparative efficiency of each school was brought out in the course of the examination, not only the children, but also the schoolmasters themselves were examined, and stimulated to exertion.

My own ^special contribution to the education of the youth of the district was the instruction of a particular class every morning. This class comprised all the children that could read with ease in the boys' and girls' day-schools and the boarding- schools in Edeyenkoody. Morning prayers were over about half- past six ; and at seven o'clock my class, generally numbering about thirty pupils, assembled. The children then read before me a chapter, or a portion of a chapter, of Scripture in order, and were questioned and instructed in its meaning. Sometimes one day was devoted to a chapter, sometimes four or five days, according to the amount of difficulty contained in it, or the de sirableness of a thorough comprehension of it; and in this manner, slowly and carefully, with successive generations of pupils, I went four times through the Gospels and the Acts of the Apostles, twice through the historical portions of the Old Testament, and twice through the Epistle to the Romans. Once a month a day was devoted to the examination of the children by written questions and answers ; and whenever I was absent as when it was my duty to visit the out-villages I appointed the most intelligent catechist or schoolmaster to take my place. Some heathen children who attended our Edeyenkoody day- schools were members of this class for several years ; and two of them, of their own accord, and through the force of real con viction of the truth, abandoned the heathenism of their families, and boldly put on Christ.

It would be needless to point out the advantages which our children must have obtained from this opportunity of being instructed so systematically in the Word of Life. For the advantages of the system to myself, also, I have no less reason to be thankful. I have often felt and said, that I learned far more Divinity in teaching my class of Tamil children every morning in Edeyenkoody, than ever I did in College when studying expressly for the Ministry. The class was over at about half-past eight or nine; and then, after taking a refreshing swim, and breakfasting, I was ready for the ordinary work of the day. My day's work varied very much in character with the varying circumstances of the time. It is the popular notion that Europeans in India go to sleep for a couple of hours in the heat of the day: this may have been the practice formerly, but the siesta is now almost unknown. The old East is at last waking up, and the handful of Englishmen that are in India, and on whom all hope for the improvement of India depend?, have too much to do to sleep in the day-time. " They that sleep" must content themselves with sleeping in the night." We cannot safely walk about in the day-time in the open sun, but we can, and do apply ourselves as closely to in-door work, and even, in certain emergencies nnd with certain pre cautions, to out-door work, as we should do in England.

Correspondence, or the examination of candidates for the sacra ments, the settlement of disputes, or inquiry into cases of discipline, brick-and-mortar work, or accounts, visiting the sick, or the administration of medicine, a service, or study, used ordinarily to occupy my time every day till the afternoon, when I was accustomed to set out to visit some village in the neighbourhood. In visiting the more distant villages I was generally out several days at a time, including two Sundays a month ; and when thus out on a tour, I always visited two villages a day. The nearer villages I visited in the evenings from Edeyenkoody ; and in thus visiting a village, it was my custom not only to assemble the Christians in church for a service and sermon, with catechization, and afterwards to enter into conversation with them, and advise and encourage them, as might be required, but also to endeavour to see and converse with the heathen of the neighbourhood, espe cially such of them as were supposed to have "ears to hear."

The Female Boarding School at Edeyenkoody seems to call for special notice, inasmuch as there was no department of missionary work carried on in the district which was more interesting or useful. This school, which was under Mrs. Caldwell's care, was partly intended as a training school for native schoolmistresses, and there are several young women usefully employed as school mistresses in various districts in Tinnevelly who were trained up in this school ; but the principal object we had in view was that of training up a certain number of the more promising daughters of our native Christians to be specimens and patterns to the rest of the people of what Christian women ought to be, and, thus, of raising the character of the female portion of the community. The pupils are admitted into the school at a very early age, be fore their habits are fully formed ; they are isolated to a great extent from native society, brought up under our own eye, under our own influence, and not only instructed in useful knowledge, but trained up in the habits and proprieties of the Christian life. We have had, at various times, in the school from thirty-five to fifty pupils, all of whom have been boarded, lodged, and clothed, as well as educated ; and they have been supported partly by the contributions of Christian friends, partly by grants from Societies, and partly by the sale of lace made by the pupils themselves. We have endeavoured to give the school, as far as possible, the cha racter of an " Industrial School," not only as a help towards making it support itself, but as a benefit to the pupils in after life ; but, notwithstanding this, its support is chiefly derived from charitable sources, and though living is peculiarly cheap in Tinnevelly, and a school of this kind may be maintained there at less expense, perhaps, than in any other part of the world, yet it must be admitted that, at the cheapest, it is an expensive species of education, and we should certainly not have established and carried on a school on so expensive a plan, had it not been for our conviction of its absolute necessity.

It had been found by other Missionaries before us, and we also found, on putting it to the test, that day-schools for girls did not fully meet the peculiar circumstances of India, and that if we wished female education to make any real progress, for one or two genera tions at least, we must rely chiefly on female boarding schools. This necessity arises out of the peculiar position of women in India, and they who have not been in India themselves will be enabled in some degree to realize this necessity, when I. explain to them familiarly what the position of Hindu women is.

A fair estimate may be formed of the civilization of a people from the treatment which their women receive. Amongst savages the women do all the hard work, and the men, when they are not fighting or hunting, are smoking, drinking, or sleeping; on the other hand, amongst the christianized, civilized nations of Europe, the highest social honours are conceded to women. The position of women in India, like the position of India in the scale of civilization, lies midway between those extreme points.

It is a mistake to suppose that Hindu women are treated like slaves, if hard work is regarded as an essential feature of slavery ; for, perhaps, in no country in the world have women less work to do than in India. They live an easy, shady life, with little to do and less to think about ; they are well fed, better clothed than the men, well hung out with jewels, rarely beaten when they don't deserve it, and generally treated like household pets. In their own opinion, they have nothing to lament as a class, but are as well treated as women could wish to be, and are perfectly content. On the other hand, if slavery means social degradation, Hindu women must be regarded as slaves ; for not only are they denied equal rights with the men, but they are regarded as having no claim to any rights or feelings at all.

The Hindu wife is not allowed to eat with her own husband ; her duty is to wait upon her husband whilst he is eating, and to eat what he has left. If they have any children, the boys eat with their father, and, after they have done, the girls eat with their mother. Nor is this the custom among the lower classes only; it is the custom amongst every class of Hindus, in every part of India where I have been. When they are assembled together on any festive occasion, you never see the women seated on the same level with the men: if there is a dais or any elevated place, the men occupy the elevation, which is the place of honour, and the women squat cross-legged on the ground, or stand. If a party are going any-where on a visit, the men always walk first, the women humbly follow ; the wife never so far forgets her place as to walk side by side with her husband, much less arm in arm. The husband, it is true, is not forgetful of his wife's comfort ; if they can afford it, a conveyance is pro vided for the female portion of the party, and the men are content to walk. Still, they generally take care to preserve their dignity by walking on in front, and the conveyance must keep behind. In the Telugu language, the language of fourteen millions of people in southern India, the relative position of the women is illustrated by the pronouns of the third person. There is no feminine pronoun no word signifying "she" in the ordinary spoken dialect ! The only pronouns of the third person com monly used are vddii, " he," and adi, c: it." " He" of course denotes the lords of the creation," and to whom or what does "it" apply ? to women and cattle and irrational things in general. Worse than all this is the circumstance that Hindu women are unable to read, and are not allowed to learn. The dancing girls connected with the greater temples, a small and very dis reputable class, are taught to read, and within the last few years, through the influence of European Christianity, female education has become more or less fashionable in such places as Calcutta and Madras ; but with these exceptions, if exceptions they are, the heathen women of India are totally uneducated. I never myself met with a heathen -woman who could read, and in thai district in the South where I laboured, and where I was well acquainted with the condition of the people, no woman, I suppose, had learned to read from the beginning of the world, till Christ ianity was introduced, and our Christian schools established. The consequence of this ignorance is, that Hindu women are exceedingly superstitious and exceedingly silly ; but instead of the men being ashamed of this silliness, they think it the normal condition of the female mind. For instance, one of their poets, in describing the excellences of various classes of people, says

"To be a simpleton is the ornament of a woman."

Nor did the poet, in uttering this sentiment, mean to be sarcastic or to excite a laugh. He uttered it in all seriousness, and thought he was saying something to which every one would assent.

What is more extraordinary still, is, that though the arts of civilized life have made much progress in India, I never met with, and never heard of, a heathen woman in India who could sew. Excellent sewing is done in India ; muslins and silks are beauti fully embroidered ; but everything of that sort is done by men. Men are the dressmakers and milliners, men are the washerwomen, men milk the cows ; in short, nearly all the work that is done by women in this country is done by men in India. What then, it may be asked, do the women do 1 They have to attend to their household affairs, they have to attend to the comfort of their families, they have to go through a good deal of religious and social ceremonial ; and this, with few exceptions, is regarded as the sum-total of their duty. The women belonging to the very lowest class in society, the class of agricultural slaves, work nearly as hard as their husbands in the fields and in the open sun ; the women belonging to the classes immediately above add a few pence a month to the family income by spinning cotton ; a few \romen also are bazaar keepers, or hawkers of cakes ; but the women belonging to the more comfortable classes and the higher classes have no occupation whatever for their spare time. The whole of their time is not occupied by the preparation of the family meal and their simple household duties ; after all this is over, much time remains at their own disposal, and as they cannot read, and cannot sew, and cannot do any sort of "work," their time hangs very heavily on their hands, and they are driven to spend a large portion of it in ceremonies or in sleep, in gossip or in scandal. We may be sure that the devil will find plenty of occupation for those idle hands and those idle tongues !

After this description of Hindu manners, the women of England will scarcely be inclined to envy the women of India. But, it may be asked, Why do women occupy in this country so different a position] It is wholly owing to the Christian religion. It is Christianity which has taught the husband to love his wife, "as Christ also loved the Church," and to give her honour as " the weaker vessel." It is to Christianity that the Christian wife is indebted for her social position ; and therefore all who value that position should be thankful to God for their Christianity, and anxious to diffuse its purifying influences throughout the earth. The condition of Hindu women generally being such as I have described, every one must at once see the necessity of special and earnest endeavours for the promotion of female education ; and at the same time, when it is borne in mind that the more ignorant any class of people are, they are the more contented with their ignorance, and that in every department of life custom is the supreme rule by which Hindu society is governed, we shall be able to form some estimate of the difficulties with which female education was found to be beset.

Even when the people had become Christians, the difficulty of inducing parents to allow their daughters to learn to read seemed for a time insuperable. " Of what use can reading be to women 1 ? it is contrary to the custom of the country, it is disreputable ; surely you don't want our daughters to resemble dancing-girls ? It is necessary, of course, that they should become Christians, and learn by heart various texts and prayers, but that is all the learning our women require. Do the women of your country learn all the sciences that men do ?" Such was the line of opposition generally taken ; and hence, if we wanted female education to make any real progress, we found it necessary to make it popular to sweeten it to the taste of the ignorant by linking to it advantages which they could appreciate to board and clothe a number of pupils, in addition to instructing them: and fortunately this very arrangement has enabled us to give the pupils a thoroughly good education such an education of mind and character, together with instruction in useful knowledge and useful employments, as should enable them to commend to their neighbours the edu cation they had received, and dissipate prejudice by the influence of their example. This is a result which the female boarding- school certainly has accomplished ; so much so, indeed, that it is retained now chiefly on account of its intrinsic usefulness, for the prejudice of our native Christians against female education has disappeared, and even in our day-schools the number of the girls bears now the natural proportion to the number of the boys.

We found it all the more necessary to labour for the promotion of female education, when we found that Hindu women, notwith standing their ignorance, are very influential in their families. It is commonly supposed, even by Europeans who have some ac quaintance with India, that Hindu women are destitute of influence ; but this is a mistake. After residing amongst them for some years, and acquiring an intimate acquaintance with their social and domestic life, we found that the majority of the married women of India are quite as influential in their families as women anywhere are. Indeed, it is inevitable that this should be the case, for whatever be their education or their intelligence, mothers have necessarily more influence than any other persons in the bringing up of their children and an influence at least equal to that of other relations in all moral and social matters affecting the interests of the family. Children are brought up in the atmosphere of their mother's influence, and though they may surpass their mother in intelligence, they are seldom able to rise above her in manners, morals, and tone of mind. Hindu women have much more influence with their husbands, also, than is com monly supposed.

Looking at the studied way in which they are assigned the lowest place in society, one would not have expected to find this to be. the case; but the fact is so, and I can only account for it on the supposition that nature is too strong for arti ficial rules. I have frequently met with Hindus who have can didly alleged as a reason for their not becoming Christians, the refusal of their wives to give their consent. In one instance a respectable farmer, who had long been kept back by his wife, determined to become a Christian without her: accordingly one day he came to church ; but his Christianity lasted one day only, for " his wife cried all night," as the native teacher of the village told me, and the poor man came to church no more. Even after people have become Christians, and promised to submit to our pastoral care, we have often found that no progress could be made in moral reforms, and little progress of any kind, if the women were not heartily on our side. Hence it will be seen how desirable it was that we should have a female boarding-school, in additon to our day-schools, and that some at least of the future wives and mothers of the district should be so taught and brought up that there might be a reasonable hope of their using their influence in their families for good.

The result has not only justified, but exceeded our expectations. It cannot be said, indeed, that every girl brought up in the school has turned out exactly what we could have wished, but the result has proved satisfactory in so large a number of instances the boarding-school has evidently been the centre and focus of so many of the reforming, purifying influences which have been at work in the district of so many of the pupils it can be said that they are the best behaved, most Christian-minded, most European-like women in the villages in which they live con sistent communicants and useful members of society that there is no department of missionary labour pursued in the district which has more amply justified the expenditure incurred in its behalf.

The expense of conducting the school has been much smaller, indeed, than might have been supposed. A school of this kind would be very expensive in England ; but money goes so far in Tinnevelly, owing to the extreme cheapness of the necessaries of life, that we have found ourselves able to educate and maintain a pupil for the small sum of 2l. 10s. per annum. Out of this sum, which amounts to a little less than a shilling a week, we can board and lodge, and clothe, and educate a pupil, from her child hood till her fifteenth or sixteenth, year, by which time her friends get her settled in life ; and we are generally able to lay by a little, even out of this small sum, to meet contingencies. One sees from, this how far a shilling will go, and how much good a shilling may do, in the Mission field of Tinnevelly.

"Whilst the school has chiefly been supported by contributions from Christian friends, and grants from Societies, it has always been our endeavour to give it the character of an Industrial School, partly in order to enable it as far as practicable to support itself, and partly to meet the want of some means of employment suitable for women, which appeared to be one of the most crying wants of the neighbourhood. Accordingly, Mrs. Caldwell set about teaching the first pupils of our Edeyenkoody boarding-school to make lace ; and the experiment has succeeded so well that lace-making has already become in Edeyenkoody a flourishing branch of manufacture, and a source of considerable and increasing profit to the school. The lace has an excellent sale the demand far exceeds the supply and, although lace-making is far from being a profitable employment in this country, our native Christian women in Tinnevelly find it very remunerative ten times more remunerative, indeed, than any other sort of employment which was open to them before, besides being a clean, becoming employ ment, peculiarly suited to the habits and capabilities of Hindu women. The quality of the lace may be judged of from this, that specimens of it were sent by the East India Company, at its expense, to the Paris Exhibition of the Industry of All Nations f and subsequently to the Art-Treasures Exhibition in Manchester, and that a medal was awarded for it to the Edeyenkoody School, as well as another to that of Nagercoil, (in which this branch of industry originated,) by the Council of the Madras Exhibition.

One important result of all this is, that the condition of the edu cated Christian young women of the neighbourhood has been very much improved. Formerly the women were totally ignorant, and generally as helpless as they were ignorant entirely dependent for their support upon their relations: now, it not unfrequently happens that a young woman is not only better educated, but actually able to earn more than her husband, or her brother; and although this is not likely to be the case universally or always, nor is it our object to bring it about, yet undoubtedly it has had a good effect in the neighbourhood, in proving to the men, that women really can learn when they are taught, that they really can turn their learning at times to some profitable account, and that female education is far from being either the chimerical or the dangerous thing they had supposed it to be. When we first began to teach girls to read and sew, and do similar unheard-of exploits, some of the men would ask us sarcastically, " Are you going to teach the cows next 1" but the tables have now been turned upon those Avho said so, and they confess that women are so like men, after all, that we were right in teaching them as we did.

Another excellent result of the success of this portion of our work is, that it has proved to the people of the neighbourhood that Christianity has " the promise of the life that now is, as well as of that which is to come," it has proved that if Christianity finds any class of the community degraded, it does not leave them as it found them, but sets about rescuing them from their de graded condition ; and this is a very important lesson for heathens and newly-converted Christians to learn.

I have mentioned that the school was partly supported by grants from

Societies, viz., by grants made by the Society or Promoting Christian Knowledge, and the Madras Diocesan Com mittee of the Society for the Propagation of the Gospel. The grants of the former Society for all such objects have ceased, and those of the Madras Committee of the latter Society through the financial difficulties with which it has had to contend for some time) have been reduced one-half ; yet, notwithstanding this curtailment of income, I am anxious not to diminish, but to increase, the number of pupils in the school, and also to establish a somewhat similar Industrial Boarding School for Boys, for the purpose of endeavouring to raise the tone of mind and character amongst the rising generation of young men. We are, therefore, under the necessity of depending more than ever upon the help of friends who are interested in the improvement of India and in the Christian education of the Hindus. The amount required for the support and education of a pupil is, as I have said, 21. 10s. per annum, and already some kind friends have sent me contributions towards this purpose. In every case in which funds are supplied for the support of a pupil, I undertake to send annually to the donor's address a special report of the condition and prospects of the school.*

There are many other details of our Tinnevelly work, besides those I have now given, which my limits will not allow me to describe. I have accomplished that which I intended if I have given a tolerably distinct idea of the general features of the interesting and important work which is being carried on. Our work in Tinnerelly is indeed a very interesting as well as a very important one, but it would be an error to suppose every portion of it to be of as cheering and encouraging a description as some of the particulars that have been mentioned. The whole picture will not bear to be painted in rose-coloured hues. Much of our work is of a very up-hill character, requiring in those who are

It may be desirable to mention here, for the information of friends -who may be so kind as to undertake to support a pupil in our Boarding School, and who wish to know how to send future contributions for this purpose, that the best way will be to remit them, from year to year, amongst the other contributions of their parish or neighbourhood, through the local Treasurer, taking care to have it stated in the accounts sent up to the Society, that it is a " Special Contribution for Edeyenkoody Boarding School.

engaged in it, much patience and love, as well as much energy. It is no easy task to induce hereditary idolaters and demonolaters to abandon their national superstitions, and to embrace a religion which is generally regarded by their fellow-countrymen with jealous}' as a foreign religion, and with dislike as a holy religion ; and even after they have been induced to embrace it after the entire inhabitants of a village, for example, have abandoned their idols and placed themselves under Christian instruction, instead of all difficulty being at an end, as some persons might too hastily suppose, the greatest difficulty of all is that which then meets our view the difficulty of training up the new Christian com munity in accordance with " the mind that was in Christ," so as to render it really worthy of the Christian name. That is a difficulty indeed ! The whole community has to be moulded into a new shape ; not only has much to be learnt, but much also has to be unlearnt. The people must be taught new habits, manners, associations, ideas, feelings the whole framework of society must be modelled anew, and in this process of re modelling, many disappointments occur many a vessel is " marred upon the wheel," and must be thrown aside as " unfit for the master's use," and it is well if the bulk of the community does not draw back to its former position. Few people but Mis sionaries know what the remodelling of a community means, or how many difficulties are involved in the process. Still, every Missionary who has been engaged in it has found all difficulties overcome in time by gentle firmness and resolute patience, by " prayer and pains." If he can but convince the people that he loves them, and that the God who sent him loves them, success is certain in the end ; and in the meantime, whilst " the care of all the churches " in his district fills his mind, whilst he is struggling with difficulties at twenty points at once, he finds in this holy war a noble, delightful excitement, a joy in battle, which is his present reward.

LECTURE 3

Having described the Field and the Work, I now proceed to give a brief estimate of the Results of our labours in Tinnevelly. The work being one in which I have taken part myself, it may be supposed to be difficult for me to give au impartial estimate of its results. It is my wish, however, and shall be my endeavour, to be impartial to tell, not how things ought to be, but how things are ; and thero are so many undoubted proofs of progress apparent in the South Indian Missions, but especially in those of Tinnevelly, that the difficulty of being impartial, and putting in the shadows where they are required, is really not so great as might be supposed.

It used to be said, that it was impossible to convert the Hindus, and they who said so, the Anglo-Indians of a former gene ration, did their best to fulfil their own prophecy by preventing Missionaries from labouring in India. Now that the possibility of the conversion of the Hindus has been proved by the conver sion of a considerable number of them, of almost every caste, the point of attack has been changed, and it is asserted that there are no sincere Christians amongst the Hindus, so that the conversions that take place from time to time are of no value. Some of the persons who make this assertion have been in India themselves ; but there are many Englishmen in India who know no more of our native Christian congregations, or of the social and inner life of either heathens or Christians, than if they had never been out of England. They are content to remain profoundly ignorant of what Missionaries are doing, and of the real condition of the native Christian community. They adopt the language which passes current in "society," and English society in India is thoroughly pervaded with the notion that every race should keep to its own creed, and that it is an ungentlemanly thing for a man to change his religion. This is a notion which high-caste heathens take much care to encourage. Their own religion makes no pro selytes, and accepts none; consequently, they regard those who have adopted a foreign religion, especially if they are guilty of the addi tional crime of being of lower caste than themselves, as " the filth of the world and the off-scouring of all things;" and hence, Euro peans who occupy official positions in India, who are surrounded by high-caste subordinates, and breathe every day of their lives an atmosphere of high-caste blandishments, too often mistake the prejudices instilled into their minds by Brahmans for results of their own observation. It is also a significant fact, a fact which, so far as I know, admits of no exceptions, that when English gentlemen of this class are awakened to spiritual life, they make the discovery that there is a reality in missionary results, and a sincerity amongst native Christians, notwithstanding their defects, which they had not expected to find. They may find, it is true, a dark side to the picture, as well as a bright one ; but they in variably admit it to have been a gross mistake to suppose, as they did, that the picture had no bright side at all.

In this country missionary labours and successes are some times exposed to the opposite danger of being over-estimated. It sometimes seems to be supposed that all our converts must have been converted not only from idolatry to Christianity, but from sin to God ; that they must all have been renewed in the spirit of their minds, and become real, spiritual Christians. A missionary station is not depicted in colours taken from daily life, but is fancied to be a sort of Garden of Eden a chosen spot of consecrated ground in which there is no ignorance, no super stition, no strife, no immorality I had almost said, no human nature. This view of the case is equally erroneous with the former, though originating in a more friendly feeling, and it is hard to say which species of exaggeration does the cause of Missions most harm. The fact is, that the work of God in heathen lands does not differ essentially from the same work at home. In Tinnevelly as in England good has to struggle with evil, truth with error, light with darkness: nowhere on earth shall we find the characteristics of heaven. They are in error who dwell upon the dark side of the picture, and ignore the bright side ; and they are equally, though more amiably, in error, who fix their eyes exclusively upon the bright side, and ignore the dark.

The work of Misions in Thmevelly is a real work, with real difficulties and real encouragements, and it only claims to be judged by the principles on which every similar work is estimated in Christian countries.

In endeavouring to form a fair estimate of the results which have really been accomplished, we are sometimes met at the outset by the statement that all our native Christians belong to low and degraded castes. The great majority of Hindu converts belong undoubtedly to the lower classes of society: in the country they are small farmers and farm labourers, not unfrequently slaves ; in the cities they are mostly domestic servants of Euro peans. But though this is the case of the majority, it is not the case with all ; and even if it were, what then ? It would only follow that in India, as in ancient Greece, not many wise, not many noble, not many mighty are called, but that God had chosen the poor of this world to be rich in faith.

Few of the English resident in India ever have the opportunity of seeing any native Christians but those who belong to the class of domestic servants, and they sometimes complain of members of that class in unmeasured terms. It is a common saying amongst the English in India, that Christian servants are worse than heathen ones ; and though I regard this assertion as false and calumnious, yet I admit that the character of persons of that class is often unfavourably affected by their position. Tried by any standard whatever, the character of the Christian members of any caste will more than bear a comparison with heathens belonging to the same caste, but if persons belonging to different castes or classes are compared, the comparison is unfair. The domestic servants of Europeans in the Madras Presidency gene rally belong to the caste of Pariars a caste which has been degraded by long-continued oppression, and which is one of the fevr castes that are accustomed to use intoxicating liquors. Pariars sometimes boast that they belong to " Master's caste," and many European masters have discovered to their cost that their Pariar servants entertain no superstitious scruples respecting meats and drinks. Unquestionably, therefore, this caste appears in some particulars at a disadvantage in comparison with some of the more temperate, more polished castes, and those of this caste who have become Christians have peculiarly strong tempta tions and many evil customs to contend with. It is an aggrava tion of the difficulty that the majority of European masters measure their servants by a stricter rule than they apply to persons who are not in their employment, and rarely take any interest in their moral and spiritual welfare, beyond maligning all native Christians when any of their domestics commit an offence. It should be remembered, on the other hand, that nineteen-twentieths of the native Christians in the Madras Presidency belong to classes considerably higher than the Pariars in the social scale ; they reside in the rural districts, and never come in contact with Europeans at all, either as domestic servants, or in any other capacity. In Tinnevelly, in particular, there are thousands of native Christian ryots who have never yet seen any European layman. In the course of my fourteen years' connexion with Tinnevelly, my own district was visited only thrice by Europeans who were not Missionaries ; and in such circumstances it is obvious that none but the Missionaries are in a position to form or to express any reliable opinion respecting the character o/ our native Christians, or even respecting their condition in life and social influences.

If it is to be regretted that the majority of our native Chris tians belong to the lower circle of castes, it is for a reason that lies deeper than anything yet mentioned.

If a man gives up anything for Christ, he receives from Christ sevenfold more in spiritual gifts and graces; he rises rapidly to the stature of a perfect man in Christ. On the contrary, if he is so situated that -he is called upon to give up little, either because he has little to give up, or because he meets with little opposition, and more especially, if he gains, on the whole, in a temporal point of view, by becoming a Christian not indeed in a pecu niary sense, for that can rarely happen, but as regards protection' from oppression, or any similar advantage the probability is that he will acquire little elevation of spirit, or enlargement of heart, and little experience of the power of faith. Individuals may, indeed, be met with, even under such circumstances, who will rise to Christian eminence ; but if there be a community in this position, like the bulk of our native community in Tinne-velly, in the first ages at least of its Christianity, that com.- munity may be expected to exemplify the truth of this state ment. On the other hand, there is nothing new in this in the history of the Christian Church, for it has ever been a character istic of Christianity, that it has delighted to preach the Gospel to the poor ; and it has ever been another of its characteristics, that it has elevated the temporal as well as the spiritual condition of those who have embraced it. It is also necessary to bear in mind, that though the majority of our native Christians belong to the poorer classes, all do not. There is a small, but steadily- increasing portion of the native Christian community in India, consisting chiefly of the high caste youth converted to Christianity in connexion with the educational department of Missions, who may be regarded as Hindu Christian gentlemen. The social rank of some members of this class is as respectable as their attainments in English scholarship ; and as they have invariably renounced caste and kindred for Christ's sake,- they have attained thereby to " great boldness in the faith" and " a good degree" in Christ's school. Such persons bear the same relation to the less educated, less distinguished majority, that the ornamented capital of a column does to the simple, solid shaft ; and not only do they furnish a reply to the objection that our native Christians belong to the lower castes alone, but they tend to raise the tone of character and feeling throughout the entire body. They are " the first- fruits unto Christ" from the higher classes of the Hindus, and they lead us to expect in due time a rich harvest of accessions from those classes to the Christian cause.

In proceeding to furnish an estimate of the results of missionary labours in Tinnevelly, I begin with temporal results, such results being the first that strike the eye of persons visiting our stations. The whole of the civilization of Northern Europe being due to Christianity, we cannot doubt the power of the Gospel to civilize a community ; it is evident too, on comparing Protestant com munities with Roman Catholic, that the civilizing power of the Gospel is in proportion to its freedom from corruption. On turning to Tinnevelly, and comparing the temporal condition of the native Christians with that of the heathens, we cannot but be struck with the visible improvement which the Gospel has effected.

In passing from village to village you can tell, without asking a question, which village is Christian, and which is heathen. You can distinguish the Christian village by such signs as these the straightness and regularity of the streets, the superior con structon and neatness and cleanness of the cottages, the double row of tulip-trees or cocoa-nut palms, planted along each street for ornament as well as for shade, and the air of humble re spectability which everywhere meets your view all so different from the filth and indecency, the disorder and neglect, which assure the visitor that a village is heathen. You notice also, as you pass through, a marked difference in the people themselves especially in the women. The Christian women are more decently attired, and more intelligent-looking than their heathen sisters ; and instead of hiding themselves on the approach of an European stranger, they come out and give him, as he passes, the Christian salutation.

In every case with which I am acquainted, villages which have held fast and valued the Christianity they received, have risen, sometimes in the first generation, always in the second, to the enjoyment of greater prosperity and comfort, and to a higher position in the social scale, than any heathen village of the same caste.

My own village of Edeyenkoody furnishes an illustration of this. For some years after my arrival the houses of the people continued to be, as all Shanar houses had always been, unfit for civilized human beings to live in: in the course of time, however, one of the villagers resolved to build a better house for himself, and gradually the movement extended and became fashionable, until at length almost every person in the village, from the richest to the poorest, has built for himself a new house ; and the new houses the people have thus built for themselves are twice or thrice as large as the houses they were content to live in before, besides being much loftier, airier, and more respectable-looking, with little verandahs in front, and various other arrangements which used to be seen only in the houses of high-caste people in the towns. There is still undoubtedly room both for architectural improvement and for sanitary improvement ; nevertheless, the changes that have already taken place are a good omen for the future, especially seeing that they have been carried into effect by the people themselves, of their own accord, and at their own expense, and are directly the results of Christian influences.

Christianity has given the people higher ideas of their capa bilities and duties, even with respect to their present life ; it has taught them self-respect, and some degree of self-reliance: it has not made them, perhaps, more industrious, for in their own quiet, apathetic way, almost all Hindus are tolerably industrious already ; but it has made them more enterprising, more energetic ; it has knocked off the fetters wherewith their intellects were bound, and bid them go forth free ; and thus it has opened before them an unlimited prospect of progress and improvement.

It may seem a low view of matters to say that it is a character istic of Christianity that it teaches people to be cleanly ; and yet, if it be true, as is proverbially said, that " cleanliness is next to godliness," it is a circumstance worth mentioning, that an in creased attention to cleanliness has invariably accompanied the reception of the Gospel in Tinnevelly. The higher classes of the Hindus have always been very cleanly, for daily ablutions are a part of their religion; but the lower classes are very filthy in their habits, and Shnars of the poorer sort are, perhaps, filthier even than castes that are lower than themselves in the social scale, which is owing to the nature of their employment, the men being climbers of the palmyra, and the women and children boilers of palmyra sugar.

When dealing with people of this and similar classes, who had agreed to place themselves under Christian instruction, I have often thought of the appropriateness of Jacob's address (Gen. xxxv. 2), " Now, therefore, put aM-ay the strange gods that are among you, and be ye clean (or bathe), and wash your garments." In the history of our Christian communities in Tinnevelly this putting away of idols and washing of the garments have always gone hand in hand, so that, though there may be room for improvement still, the external appearance of our people, especially when assembled in church, is so much more respectable than that of their heathen neighbours, they are so much cleaner and brighter-looking, that they would inevitably be supposed by a stranger to be of higher caste than they are.

This improvement, like every improvement of an outward and visible character, is especially apparent in our young people. I wish I could take you, my dear reader, to Edeyenkoody on a Sunday, and enable you to se6 for yourself the degree in which our young people are improved. Though you cannot speak a word of the native language, and are unable to ask any person a question, yet, if you only use your eyes, you cannot but be con vinced that Christianity has proved a remarkable blessing to the rising generation. There they are, sitting in the front rows on either side ; and they are evidently, as a class, in advance of the older people. You see them better dressed and cleaner-looking, to begin with: then also they are evidently more intelligent; generally they have softer and more amiable looks ; they have books in their hands, and when a question is put by the preacher, it is from them that the answer generally proceeds ; they have the praises of God in their lips ; and there is an air about them which bespeaks them to be the Church's children, "born in her house." They owe these signs of superiority to the education they have received, for they have been brought up from the beginning in Christian knowledge and Christian habits, whereas most of the older people whom you see sitting behind, were converted from heathenism late in life, and have rarely lost the stains and rust of their original condition.

The progress of the Christian community will be very satisfac tory, if each generation gets as far ahead of the previous one as the rising generation has already outstripped the past. We cannot expect in a single generation all the results, whether temporal or spiritual, which we aim at. We have learnt that God "visits the iniquities of the fathers upon the children unto the third and fourth generation." Now, neither the fourth nor even the third generation of native Christians worthy of the name, has, as yet, come and gone ; at most we are dealing now only with the second generation of Tinnevelly Christians. It is to be expected, there fore, that some of the results of the poison of a hundred previous generations of heathenism should still remain, and that the Christianity of India, how far soever superior to heathenism, should appear more or less marred or vitiated ; but if each generation rises superior to the one that went before, we shall have every reason not only to be content, but to thank God, and take courage.

We may arrive at a safe conclusion respecting the reality and sincerity, on the whole, of the Christianity of Tinnevelly, from the liberality with which the native converts contribute to religious and charitable purposes. This is everywhere a tolerably fair criterion, if not of piety towards God, at least of love to man and religious zeal. People will not give their money for the ex tension of a system in which they do not believe, or in which they take no interest. This is a rule on which we may place special reliance in India, for the Hindus are notoriously a penurious, hoarding people: generally a Hindu is as reluctant to give his money as he is to shed his blood ; and one scarcely ever hears of a debt being paid before the payment of it is enforced. This being the case, if Hindu converts, and especially if converts from demonolatry a system of gloom and hate, in which the charities of life have no place have learnt to open their hearts and hands and contribute liberally to the support of religious and charitable Societies, it must be concluded that the Gospel has really taken root amongst them, and begun to bring forth fruit ; nor will the force of this argument be much weakened by the fact that, in Tinnevelly, as elsewhere, the amount of a particular donation is sometimes determined, not by the importance of the object, but by the amount which neighbours have given ; and that there, as in the primitive Churches and amongst ourselves, it is occasionally necessary to say, " Let every man do according as he is disposed in his heart, not grudgingly or of necessity, for God loveth a cheerful giver."

In Tinnevelly religious and charitable Societies have been es tablished in each of our districts for almost every purpose we wish to accomplish ; and those Societies depend for support, not upon Europeans, for there are no

Europeans resident in the rural districts, but upon the native Christians themselves. In my own district, for instance, I had a Church Building Society, and a Society for the Relief of the Christian poor, both independent of other districts, besides an Association connected with the Tinne velly Tract and Book Society, and one connected with the Bible Society; and since I left Tinnevelly another Society has been com menced, in my own as in most other districts, for the diffusion of the Gospel by native itinerants amongst the neighbouring heathen.

I am unable to state the precise sum- total of the various charitable contributions raised in Tinnevelly, amongst the native Christians of all the districts connected with both Missions, but the best estimate I have been able to form is that it amounts to 1,1 00. sterling a-year. I can state with certainty the exact amount raised in my own district ; and in this, as in other things, there was so much emulation at work, that there was little difference between one district and another, allowance being made for difference in numbers and worldly circumstances. Leaving out of account whatever contributions I may have re ceived from Missionaries and other European friends, I find that the native Christians of my own district contributed 12QL to their various societies and charities, during the two years that elapsed before I left Tinnevelly. This sum also, handsome as it is, must be estimated at far more than its apparent value ; for the value of money depends, not upon its weight or tale, but upon its relation to food. At the Gold Diggings a pound will scarcely purchase half as much of the necessaries of life as in England ; consequently, a donation of a pound given to a Mel bourne Society must be reckoned as one of ten shillings only. On the other hand, the value of money is much greater in India than in England. As estimated by the average price of rice in India, compared with the average price of wheat in England, I reckon the value of money in India to be seven to one six to one perhaps in some districts, at least seven to one in Tinnevelly: that is, one pound will purchase seven pounds' worth of food ; consequently, a donation of one pound to a Tinnevelly Society must be reckoned as one of seven pounds. By food, I under stand, of course, such food as is necessary to natives of the place, whose constitutions are adapted to the climate. Some things are regarded as necessaries of life by Europeans, which most Hindus have not yet learnt to regard even as luxuries. Thus, it is necessary for an European in India to have an airy house to live in, to have the means of locomotion without exposure to the sun, and also to sit on chairs, not cross-legged on the floor, and to eat with knives and forks, not with the fingers. It is necessary for an Englishman, except for some brief emergency, to have with him wherever he resides the principal appliances of civilized life, and all those appliances, of whatever sort they are, are more ex pensive in India than in England ; so that the estimate I have given is inapplicable to Europeans. Looking, however, exclu sively at the wants of the native at his natural wants and at the very limited range of his artificial wants, the estimate of the value of money which I have deduced from the price of grain is certainly a correct one, and a similar conclusion may be drawn from a comparison of the rate of wages paid in India and in England respectively, to agricultural labourers. A good agricultural labourer in Tinnevelly will think himself well paid at a shilling a week ; and, if he has no family, he will proba'bly manage to live at the rate of sixpence a week, and thus lay by half his wages. A man with an income of ten shillings a week is regarded as a gentleman ; but I was not fortunate enough to have any such gentlemen in my congregations. All my own people belonged to the class of small very small farmers, hired palmyra-climbers, and farm-servants, or slaves ; and though most of the farmers were owners of the lands they cultivated, I do not think there was a single native Christian in the district, whose income averaged more than five shillings a week.

It is necessary to bear these things in mind, in forming an estimate of the liberality of our native Christians. If we must multiply by seven to find the equivalent value of their incomes, we are bound also to multiply by seven to find the English equi valent of their contributions to charitable Societies. Estimated by this rule, the 120l. contributed in two years amount to 840, and this being the case, it must be admitted, I think,, that the religious sincerity of the mass of our Tinnevelly Christians has been proved by an unanswerable argument. "W ithout confound ing liberality in almsgiving with Christianity, it is evident that Christianity must have taken deep root amongst our people to produce the fruit of such liberality as I have described. May I not say, indeed, on comparing that liberality with the average amount contributed to religious and charitable Societies in many parishes in this old Christian country, that in the sandy plains and pal myra forests of Tinnevelly, Christendom is furnished with a new illustration of the prophetic axiom, " there are last that shall be first?" I have said that we have public meetings in Tinnevelly, as in this country, in aid of our various religious and charitable asso ciations, and certainly those public meetings are remarkably well attended. Not long ago, if you observed bands of villagers men, women, and children dressed in their holiday attire, and all threading in the same direction the pathways through the fields, you \vould naturally have concluded that they were going to attend some heathen festival, and that the plantains, baskets of sugar-candy, and other articles of produce they were carrying with them, were intended to be laid at the feet of the idol. In many extensive districts in the South it would now be unsafe to form this conclusion. You would probably find, on inquiry, that the people you saw were all going to attend a sangam a public meeting connected with one of our Societies and that the articles they were carrying with them were intended to swell the col lection at the public meeting.

The last meeting I attended in Tinnevelly, the meeting of the Tract, Book, and Bible Association connected with my own district, was held at Edeyenkoody, a few weeks before I left. It was held in the middle of the day, and all who attended the meeting had to give up some portion of their day's work those who came from a considerable distance an entire day's work in order to enable them to attend it. There had been heavy rain also for several days before the meeting was held, there was rain on the day of the meeting, and there was rain upon the meeting itself, for the large temporary church in which the meeting was held was in a leaky condition. Notwithstanding these various discouragements, there were upwards of 800 persons of all ages present on the occasion, all of them native Christians connected with the district. Surely this looks as if the people generally, however defective they may be in some things, had learned to take an interest in the spread of Christianity.

On the occasion referred to, some fifteen men, agricultural slaves, belonging to a village eleven miles off, came to bid me good-by after the meeting was over. I saw that there were none of the women of their village with them, and rather wondered at this; for there, as here, there is generally a larger number of women than of men present at such meetings. I asked them why this had happened. They answered, " The river was swollen ; so the women were obliged to turn back, but we swam." " Oh, you swam the river, did you 1 " I said. " Yes," said they ; " and we wish to set off at once, for we want to cross the river again before it is quite dark." Thus, those poor people walked in all twenty-two miles that day, and swam a river twice, in order to enable them to attend the meeting! Making all due allowance for difference in climate and in mode of life, I think I may fairly say that the practical interest those poor Hindu rustics took in the propagation of Christian truth, though not directly a proof of their piety, was at least a proof that in them the good seed had found a good promising soil, in which fruits of faith and labours of love were likely to grow apace.

I come now to more directly spiritual results of the reception of the Gospel. It is admitted that Christian profession and Scriptural knowledge, docility and liberality, though excellent things after their kind, may fall ahort of spiritual life. It is desirable, therefore, to inquire whether, and to what extent, our native Christian community in Tinnevelly has been endowed with spiritual life from on high. Amongst our native Christians such spiritual life as operates mightily in " works of faith, and labours of love, and patience of hope," is certainly rare and I fear, it must be added, it is rare in this country too. It is a gift of special grace, possessed not by the " many " who are " called," but by the "few " who are " chosen." If we look around us, and scrutinize the condition of even the best-managed and most enlightened parishes in England, we shall discover in them a mixture of good and evil; we shall find the best portion of every community the smallest. If we look into the description of the spiritual condition of the primitive Churches given us in the New Testament, we shall discover even in them a very mixed state of things chaff mingled with wheat in the Gospel thrashing- floor, bad fish mingled with good in the Gospel net ; we shall discover the existence of a similar mixture, in ever varying pro portions, in every century of the history of the Church. Every where nominal Christianity has accompanied real Christianity, and everywhere real Christians have been a " little flock." This state of things was clearly predicted by the Divine Founder of Christianity himself.

Look, for example, at our Lord's prophetic parable of the sower. According to that parable, one portion only of the good seed of the word " brings forth fruit unto perfection," three-fourths of all the seed that is sown are lost. One portion falls by the wayside, and is trodden under foot ; another portion falls on a good, but a shallow soil, and though it springs up speedily, it speedily whithers away ; a third portion is choked with thorns ; a fourth portion alone finds a good soil, the soil of " a good and honest heart," a heart specially prepared by Divine grace for the reception of the good seed, and it is in that soil alone that the good seed not only takes root, but grows, and brings forth fruit " in some sixty, and in some an hundred-fold."

Now, no exception to this state of things is furnished by Indian Missions in general, or by our Tinnevelly Missions in particular. We miorht wish, indeed, that all our native Christians had embraced Christianity purely and solely from a conviction of its Divine origin, and of the suitableness of its blessings to their spiritual wants, without being influenced by its collateral, tem poral advantages; we might hope also that they would never forget " the wormwood and the gall" of their inherited heathenism, or " the exceeding great love of their Master and only Saviour " in dying for their redemption; we might hope that all who abandoned heathenism would also abandon sin, that all who were converted to Christianity would also be converted to God, that all who became Christians in a heathen country would become real Christians, really renewed in the spirit of their minds, filled with real love and zeal, Christians likely, to rise speedily to "the stature of perfect men in Christ;" this and much more we might hope for, and even expect ; but the reality, though quite in accordance with what Scripture and our European experience in dicate, is little in accordance with such bright expectations. The many, in our Tinnevelly Missions, walk, as the many have ever walked everywhere, in the broad easy way of worldly compliances, and they who adorn the doctrine of God their, Saviour, are the few. On looking round us in Tinnevelly, we shall find no lack of merely nominal Christianity ; and yet here I must draw a dis tinction between what we call nominal Christianity in Tinne velly, and much that is called^by that name in England, but which appears to me to have no right whatever to the name.

In this old Christian country, especially in our crowded cities, many of those who call themselves " Christians," never enter a place of Christian worship, never bow the knee to God in prayer, never open God's word, know nothing of God except as a name to swear by. Such persons have no right even to the name of Christians, and when they are called by that name it can only mean that they are not Mahometans or Buddhists. In Tinne- velly such persons would not be called Christians at all ; their names would be erased from our Church-lists, and Christianity would not be discredited by the supposition that they are hers. When we speak of nominal Christianity in Tinnevelly, we speak of something which has a certain right to the Christian name. Our nominal Christians come to church, they send their children to school, they have abandoned their idols, they have formally placed themselves under Christian instruction, and under our pastoral care ; they have come within the sound of the Gospel, and within the range of holy influences ; they contribute to the funds of our various Societies ; they submit to a discipline in a remark ably docile manner; many of them have applied for, and received baptism, some of them come regularly to the commu nion ; in short, a considerable number of our " nominal Chris tians" would be reckoned very good Christians, and very good church-people too, in some parishes in England ; and if we call them "nominal" Christians merely, it is because we have not seen in them what we have longed to see " the power of godliness," the new life of real, spiritual Christianity and find it necessary to distinguish them from that much smaller, but much more interesting class of native Christians, who show that they are animated by the spirit of Christ.

I am not disposed to think lightly of the value of such nominal Christianity as I have described. A great and very important work has been done, when so many as 43,000 people in one pro vince of heathen India have been brought thus far, though it should be thus far only, towards the heavenly Zion. The altar has been built, the wood is piled upon the altar, the offering which St. Paul speaks of " the offering up of the Gentiles," has been placed upon the wood, and it only remains for the fire of Divine grace to descend and kindle the whole into a flame.

I am aware that there are some persons who think the ex tension of a nominal Christianity amongst heathens as no benefit at all, but a positive evil, and who withhold their sympathy from any system of Missions but that which professes only (with very doubtful success, however,) to " gather in the elect." I not only think that idea erroneous, but I regard it as a mischievous error. A religion which is merely nominal and external will not, it is true, save any man's soul ; but if our country were not a nominally Christian one, inhabited by a church-going, Bible-taught people, how much more seldom would real religion be met with 1 Suppose that large numbers of our unspiritual, unconverted countrymen were to abandon the profession of Christianity, cease attending church, throw away their Bibles, withdraw from the company of their Christian fellow-countrymen, and return in a body to th heathenism of their Saxon forefathers, would this apostasy be better or worse than their nominal Christianity ? would there be a greater or a less probability of real religion eventually making progress amongst them ? or would not they who now regard the extension of nominal Christianity in India as a doubtful benefit or as a positive evil, speak loudly and warmly of the importance of even an external profession of Christianity 1 If this case is correctly put, why should we have one law for Europeans and another for our dealings with a people who are lower in intellect, in civilization, and in religious development, and who are there fore more likely, in their progress to real religion, to pass through the stage of nominal religion ? Instead, therefore, of that morbid dread of the extension of nominal Christianity which some good people evince, it should simply be our desire and prayer that "the power of godliness" may become co-extensive with the "form" of it, and that the "dry bones" of heathenism may not only be clothed with sinews, and flesh, and skin, but vivified and raised up by the Divine " breath. ' It is greatly to be deplored that any persons, whether Europeans or Hindus, should remain content with the empty form, without the substance of godliness ; and it should therefore be regarded as a special consolation, that we who have laboured in Tinnevelly as Missionaries and as pastors, who " speak what we do know, and testify what we have seen," are able to testify that there is in Tinnevelly, not only much of a vague general profession of religion, but an encouraging amount of genuine piety. In each of our little congregations God has "a seed to serve Him." There is " a little flock," would that I could say they are not a little flock ! of persons who appear to be " called, and faithful, and chosen followers of the Lamb ; and such persons show the reality of their religion by the regularity of their attendance on the means of grace, by their zeal in the acquisition of religious knowledge, by the quiet consistency of their lives, by their devout confidence in God's care, by their conquest over their caste-preju dices, by the largeness of their charities, and in a variety of other ways which are quite satisfactory to their pastors' minds. The existence of this class of persons, though they are still a minority everywhere, is an immense encouragement to the Christian Mis sionary ; for it proves to him that the Gospel has not waxed old has not become effete, as some people affirm but is still, as in primitive times, "the power of God, and the wisdom of God" to the salvation of every one that believeth: it proves that Chris tianity is not merely a new dogma, or a new society, but new love, new life ; not merely a new patch upon an old garment, or a new garment upon " the old man," but the creation of " a new man" in Christ Jesus.

The existence of a considerable amount of real Christian piety amongst our native Christians, may be inferred from the number of our communicants.

In almost every portion of our Tinnevelly Missions, the proportion apparent between the communicants and the baptized part of the Christian population is very remarkable. Amongst a Christian population of about 43,000 souls, about a third of whom are still unbaptized, the communicants amount, in round numbers, to 5,000. This gives a proportion of about one communicant to every six baptized persons throughout the province. In some villages with which I am acquainted, the pro portion is one in five ; and if there are not at least one in eight of the baptized inhabitants of a village communicants, that is, if there are not at least 100 communicants in a village of 800 baptized inhabitants we are accustomed to think the religious condition of that village deplorably low. We should form, it is true, an erroneous impression of the religious prosperity of Tinnevelly if we looked at these facts from a purely English point of view. The Hindus, and other semi- civilized races, have so much less mental independence and self- reliance than the English, and when disposed to act right are so much more teachable, tractable, and submissive, that a pastor's recommendation carries greater weight, and his influence produces greater effect than is ordinarily the case in English congregations. Hence, if we take an English congregation and an Indian one, which are equal in numbers, and equal, as far as man can judge, in the aggregate amount of their piety and zeal, we shall gene rally find a considerable inequality in the number of the com municants.

In estimating the value of facts like this, differences in mental temperament are certainly to betaken into account; nevertheless, we should not be doing justice to our Missions if we did not attribute a considerable share of the difference to the system pursued. Our people may be more docile than the English, but our system also is better.. It is not the custom in any of our missionary stations, as it generally is in England, for people to come to the Lord's Table when they please, and keep away when they please, without any reference to character or preparation, coming unprepared and going away unblessed. We have a " godly discipline," and a regular system of instruction and training, similar to that which in this country precedes Confirmation, but generally a good deal stricter. At all our stations in Tinnevelly, on the Saturday preceding the administration of the Holy Com munion, we are accustomed to hold " a preparation," or preparatory meeting, which all who wish to partake of the Communion, are expected to attend. From a distance of four or five miles people attend this meeting almost as a matter of course, but people who live at greater distances are indulged with subsidiary " pre parations " nearer home. At these meetings the Missionary con verses with the intending communicants, catechizes them, explains to them whatever requires to be made clear, prays with them if need be, warns and exhorts them, or comforts and strengthens them, privately and endeavours in every way he can think of, to prepare them for the reception of the Holy Communion with a right faith, a reverent mind, and a lively hope. It might be expected that the strictness of this system would deter com municants, and yet, so far from deterring them, nothing seems so effectually to increase their number ; for persons who would not think themselves fit to come to the Communion itself, feel no scruple about attending the communicants' class, and thus they are gradually led on " from strength to strength," till in due time they venture to come to the Table of the Lord.

During the last six months that elapsed before I left Tin- nevelly, wishing to leave behind me something that might be useful in my absence, I reduced to a connected shape the prayers, iustructions, and meditations which I had been accustomed to supply to my people, month by month, at the preparatory meetings, and gave the whole for publication to our Tinnevelly Book Society. The book was adopted and published by the Book Society, and an edition of 3,000 copies of it printed at the Church Mission Press in Palamcottah. May I not say that this is a fact which speaks volumes t In a province where devils were the principal objects of worship, " where Satan's seat was," 3,000 copies of a book intended for the guidance and edification of Christian communicants have been called for, and have been printed and sold. Surely this may be regarded as proving that Christian piety must have made real progress. Allowing a certain abatement for the mental temperament of the people, and for the results of systematic preparation, what remains is so considerable and encouraging, as to warrant our saying, " what hath God wrought '"

In my own district the number of communicants was at first very small. For two years, amongst about a thousand native Christians there was only one person, in addition to a few catechists and schoolmasters, to whom I felt myself at liberty to administer the Communion. Those were days of darkness and dreariness indeed, and I well remember sometimes saying to myself, " Lord, I am left alone." But it was God's will that I should not always be left alone. After the schools came into full operation, and especially after the pupils who had been educated in our Female Boarding School began to take their places in our various congregations, as Christian wives and mothers, a great improvement began to take place, and by and by I found myself surrounded with a band of men and women but especially of women whose hearts God appeared to have touched.

On the whole, therefore, I conclude, from my own experience as well as from the experience of my Missionary brethren in Tinnevelly, that real piety towards God does exist amongst our people, and is the same in kind, if not in degree, with what we observe in more highly-favoured communities. We cannot expect Hindu piety to be identical in all respects with English piety, but we may expect, and we actually find, that Hindti piety is as sincere and real, after its own fashion, as English, and as much superior to the merely nominal religion by which it is sur rounded. Many a person in Christian England, though without God in the world, and without a particle of love for the Saviour who died for him, exemplifies by his high sense of honour and gentlemanly integrity, what the indirect influences of many ages of Christianity can effect: place beside him a recent convert from heathenism, and though the latter has been awakened to spiritual life by a vital spark from on high, and be sincerely desirous of following his Saviour, it is well if he does not suffer in our estimation from comparison with one who has so greatly the advantage of him in point of external circumstances. In estimating the sincerity of the real Hindu Christian, we should compare him, therefore, not with the nominally Christian English man, still less with the real English Christian, the highest style of man, but with the nominally Christian Hindu, or with the subtle, cringing, apathetic, conscienceless heathen himself, the inheritor of the concentrated poison of a hundred generations of heathenism. The Gospel does not all at once eradicate natural disposition and national failings. Our Indian converts, though they have become Christians, have not become Englishmen ; they remain Hindus still, and that means much. But whatever their failings may be, a counteracting impulse has been brought to bear upon them, and they have yielded themselves to that impulse, so that I have no fear respecting the final result. Both " the leaven" and " the lump" may be inferior to what we have now in England ; but the difference between the Indian leaven and the Indian lump is equally marked and decided, and we may regard it as equally certain that in due time the lump will be pervaded by the leaven. The Indian leaven itself also is probably destined to improve in strength and virtue.

It is well known that many of the tribes of Northern Europe were converted to Christianity by the sword, or by other methods not more creditable to any party concerned in the conversion, and that the Christianity thus introduced was deeply tinged with the superstitions and errors of the times ; yet in a few centuries the Christian leaven wrought so mightily as to purify itself from the impurities and corruptions which had originally been combined with it, and to form in the northern nations a manliness and truthfulness of Christian character, previously unknown in the world. Reasoning from analogy, in a district where the people have received the Gospel from, on the whole, a higher order of motives, where the faith introduced is that which was " once de livered to the saints," without superstitious admixtures, and where the Holy Scriptures are freely distributed, and the Scrip tural education of the young is universal, we have surely reason to expect that the heavenly leaven will, sooner or later, work in a not less effectual manner, and with not less happy results.

When a person learns, on first becoming acquainted with Tin- nevelly, that the greater number of the native converts em braced the Christian religion either from secular motives, or from a mixture of motives, partly secular, partly religious, and when he notices the imperfections and faults which are apparent in the majority, he may conclude as some have naturally, but too hastily concluded, that all the religion of the province is unreal. In this instance, as in many others, a little knowledge leads to an erroneous conclusion, a more thorough knowledge reveals results that are as satisfactory and encouraging as the circumstances of the case will admit of.

The real state of things may be illustrated by a beautiful analogy drawn from the betel gardens of India. The betel leaf is the smooth, pungent, aromatic leaf of a climbing plant, somewhat resembling the pepper-vine, which, is almost universally chewed by Orientals, not as a narcotic, but as a mild agreeable stimulant. The betel-vine is a delicate and tender plant, which, requires much water and much shade ; and, accordingly, it is trained, not up a naked pole, like the hop, but up the stem of a rapidly growing, straight, slim, leafy tree, called in Tamil the agatti, which is planted thickly in rows throughout the betel garden, so as both to give the betel the support it needs, and to screen it from the scorching rays of the sun, by the continuous shade of its inter mingling branches. At a distance, and to a casual observer, the agatti alone is apparent, and it might be supposed that we were looking at an agatti garden, not at a betel garden ; but inter spersed among the agattis, planted in the same soil, and fed by the same water, is another and more precious plant, whose wind ing tendrils and smooth green leaves attract our notice when we have entered the garden, and begun to look closely around. It is only for the sake of screening and sweetening the betel that the agatti is grown, and when the betel-leaf is ripe, the agatti which supported and defended it is cut down, and either applied to some trivial use, or cast into the fire. Thus it is in our missions in Tinnevelly, and in the visible Church in general, which in every country is a betel garden, in which " the many " who are " called," attract more notice than " the few " who are " chosen," though they are of infinitely less value, and in which " the few " grow up amongst " the many," undistinguished from them except by the close observer, and are trained up for heaven, in green, and fruitful humility, under their protecting shade.*

It is quite certain that God has not left Himself in Tinnevelly, or in any other place where his word has been preached, and his Church planted, without witnesses to the saving efficacy of his truth. Whilst He causes " the Gospel of the kingdom " to be " preached in all nations for a witness unto them," it is evidently his design that it should not ordinarily or always be a witness against them ; for He has been pleased in so many instances to accompany it with " the demonstration of his Spirit and of power," as to prove to all nations that Christianity is from God, and a remedy for the spiritual diseases of the Hindus, as well as of all other races of men.

www.ingramcontent.com/pod-product-compliance
Lightning Source LLC
Chambersburg PA
CBHW060421290526
45791CB00002B/843